THE KEY TO
CRYSTALS

THE KEY TO

CRYSTALS

FROM HEALING TO DIVINATION
ADVICE AND EXERCISES
TO UNLOCK
YOUR MYSTICAL POTENTIAL

SARAH BARTLETT

FAIR WINDS

Quarto is the authority on a wide range of topics.

Quarto educates, entertains and enriches the lives of our readers—enthusiasts and lovers of hands-on living.

www.QuartoKnows.com

First published in the United States of America in 2015 by
Fair Winds Press, a member of
Quarto Publishing Group USA Inc.
100 Cummings Center
Suite 406-L
Beverly, Massachusetts 01915-6101
Telephone: (978) 282-9590
Fax: (978) 283-2742
www.quarrybooks.com

10 9 8 7 6 5 4 3 2 1

ISBN: 978-1-59233-711-8

Digital edition published in 2015
eISBN: 978-1-62788-760-1

Conceived, designed and produced by
Quid Publishing
Part of The Quarto Group
Level 4 Sheridan House
Hove BN3 1DD
England

Design and layout by Clare Barber
Illustrations by Joanna Kerr

Printed in China

TO MY FAMILY AND FRIENDS, AND ALL THE OTHER
GEMS IN MY LIFE.

CONTENTS

CHAPTER THREE:

O—☛ The Key to Crystals
and Divination   82

CHAPTER FOUR:

O—☛ The Key to Crystals
and Healing   130

INTRODUCTION

For thousands of years crystals and stones have adorned princesses, prophets, kings, and warriors. They have also been used as divination tools and to invoke powerful healing energy. The ancient Babylonian astrologers believed that white quartz crystals harnessed the power of the constellations to determine the future, while the Egyptians used stones such as obsidian to protect the wearer from evil. In fact, crystals are the most natural, yet empowering force we can work with to help unlock our own mystical powers.

THE MAGIC OF THE UNIVERSE

My own discovery of the magic of stones began when I was sitting on a pebble beach in southern England one windy spring day when I was in my late twenties. I had just been getting over a rather dramatic love affair and, feeling relieved that life wasn't so bad after all, I had begun to "get back to nature" and take pleasure in the countryside, the sea, and the wild weather. As a child I had been taught feng shui skills by my Chinese "amah"—a kind of mother's help—when I lived in the Far East, and I had come to the seashore to gather shells and stones to help me to balance the energy of my new home. One stone "drew" me to it like a magnet. It was a jet black ovoid pebble, smooth and shiny because it was still wet from seawater. Some work of nature had etched two fine lines around its edges. The two elliptical lines crossed one another, and suddenly words came to my mind: "Trust in the magic of the Universe." So I did. As I write, this simple but beautiful stone of magical and natural power sits beside me on my desk.

Stones and pebbles are part of nature's magic, just as you are.

YOUR JOURNEY WITH CRYSTALS

You too can discover this magic. By following the fun, simple, and interactive lessons and exercises in this book, uniquely created to help you unlock your own mystical potential, you can find out all there is to know about crystals.

Chapter One reveals the basics and practicalities of working with crystals, including a brief overview of crystal power and history, as well as a step-by-step guide to choosing and caring for crystals. On every spread there is an exercise or lesson, which not only gradually builds up your own mystical powers, but also helps you to connect to the power of crystal energy.

Chapter Two shows you how to harness and interpret the attributes and qualities of the most well-known and important crystals for enhancing relationships and romance, business and careers, and the home.

Chapter Three develops your intuitive skills by working with crystals for divination. From learning how to dowse with a crystal pendulum to using crystals in special spreads to divine the future, this part of the book is devoted to teaching you to interpret the cosmic language being spoken to you by the crystals.

Chapter Four, the final chapter, looks at crystal healing and how to practice it. These exercises tone up your own body/ mind/spirit connection and enhance your alignment with the crystal energies. The major areas covered are emotional healing, life enhancement, and spiritual development. By understanding crystals and working with their powers, you too can discover the hidden energy of the cosmos that flows through you.

CHAPTER ONE

THE KEY
to
CRYSTAL
POWER

O━► Crystals are "living" stones

O━► Choosing crystals empowers
you with beneficial energy

O━► The ancients used crystals for
healing and divination

O━► Treat your crystals as you
would your friends

WHAT ARE CRYSTALS?

The Earth came into existence millions of years ago when swirling clouds of gas formed into a dense pool of dust. This dense dust bowl contracted until it finally became a white-hot ball of molten magma. The outer layer of this ball-like furnace cooled into a crust to become the Earth's mantle, the thick outer surface. Yet even now, deep within the mass of the Earth, the mineral-rich molten magma continues to boil. Not far below the surface, fiery gases and liquid magma penetrate the crust to meet solid rock. As they cool they solidify, continually forming new crystals.

LIVING STONES

Crystals are classified by their internal structure, a blueprint unique to that "type" of crystal, and a record of the powerful forces that shaped it. Quartz crystal, for example, has a totally different internal structural pattern to topaz or garnet. Some crystals are formed by the forces of water or liquids, others by erosion; some arise from the explosion of fiery gases and molten magma from the center of the Earth. Some crystals form in a matter of days; others can take hundreds of years. For example, peridot is created quickly at high temperature from liquid magma.

However, when magma slowly penetrates fissures in the bedrock, as it cools, it lays down large crystals such as amethyst. The agates are formed from layers of quartz laid in bands.

Some crystals can take hundreds of years to form, while others are laid down instantly at high temperatures from magma.

Obsidian is formed by the sudden cooling of molten lava, which means it has no time to "crystalize," giving it a dark, matte black, or umber look when unpolished. The absorption of various minerals gives rise to the wide variety of colors for every classification of crystal. At the heart of every inert-looking crystal is a constantly vibrating molecular structure. It is this vibrational frequency that makes it a "living stone."

POWERFUL ENERGY

All crystals and gemstones vibrate to what is known as the piezoelectric effect, discovered by French physicist and chemist Pierre Curie (1859–1906). What happens in a technical sense is that when mechanical stress is applied to the crystal, a voltage is produced across the crystal's surface. In fact, when you hold a crystal tightly in your hand and "warm it up," you are doing exactly that— applying stress so that its electromagnetic force comes alive. This effect is reversible, and if the polarity of the voltage is alternated, the crystal will rapidly expand and contract, producing a vibration. This is the key to the way quartz watches work.

So, an "alive" yet dormant crystal carries powerful Earth energy. Yet like everything in the Universe it is also infused with the divine force that permeates all. This electromagnetic energy, or invisible force, is the bridge between its resonance both to you and the Universe. Of course, crystals can be used merely for decorative purposes and personal adornment, but they are also important for enhancing you and your environment, for protection, attraction and banishment, for bringing love into your life, and for healing and divination.

Quartz watches and clocks vibrate to the piezoelectric effect due to an alternating frequency of voltage.

CRYSTALS IN HISTORY

Whether used as adornments, for protection, divination, or healing, throughout history gemstones and crystals have been an essential part of every culture's fascination with the Earth's unique riches and power. It is this power that you are going to learn to harness for yourself.

IN ANCIENT TIMES

As long ago as 4000 BCE, the ancient Sumerians used astrology and the stars to predict the future. They also believed that crystals were linked to planetary energy and that they reflected cosmic vibrations. They were therefore used extensively in magic formulas and spells.

The ancient Egyptians used crystals and gemstones for magical protection, to improve health, and for cosmetic purposes. Lapis lazuli was particularly revered, both as a symbol of the heavens and for its exquisite blue color. It was crafted to decorate the eyebrows on the funeral mask of King Tutankhamen (1341–1323 BCE). The color of gems was particularly significant to ancient Egyptians. The red of jasper represented fire, life, and blood; the green of malachite represented new growth and fertility, and was often included in tombs or burial chambers to represent the deceased's heart and its regenerative powers in the afterlife. It has even been speculated that the Egyptian pyramids were capped with crystals to channel cosmic forces down into the geometric structures.

In ancient Greece, fortune-telling was performed by seers who looked at the patterns of swarms of birds or the ripples in a pool, and also cast crystals to predict the future.

Crystals such as turquoise, lapis, and malachite were used to adorn the funeral masks of pharaohs such as Tutankhamen.

KEYNOTE

The ancient Greek name for amber was elektron, meaning bright sun. According to myth, when Phaëton, son of the sun god Helios, was killed, his mourning sisters became poplar trees, and their falling tears were thought to be amber, the bright teardrops of the sun's daughters.

The Greeks also believed amethyst would prevent drunkenness. Goblets were made of the crystal and hardened drinkers often wore the crystal as an amulet to stave off intoxication and hangovers. Another ancient Greek belief was that every piece of clear quartz crystal is a fragment of the mystical "Universal Crystal of Truth." They thought that it was water frozen by the gods and called it crystallos, meaning icicle. The Romans used to carry pieces of clear quartz during the summer to keep their hands cool.

Gemstone rings have been worn as protective amulets since pre-biblical days.

PROTECTION AND DIVINATION

In the Roman tradition, aquamarine was washed up on the shore from the secret jewelry boxes of sea nymphs who had stolen the sacred stones from Neptune, the god of the oceans. Ancient sailors wore aquamarine talismans engraved with Neptune's symbol as protection against dangers at sea.

The protective energy of gemstones such as topaz, emeralds, and rubies were mentioned in the Old Testament Book of Exodus. Twelve different gemstones were embedded in the breastplate of the High Priest of the Israelites and were believed to give the wearer divine power and protection. In pre-Columbian Meso-American cultures, the Aztecs polished black obsidian to make mirrors, which they used to see into the future. The sixteenth-century English astrologer and magus Dr. John Dee owned such a mirror, which he used to call up angelic powers. The Mayans also used jade beads infused with supernatural power for scrying, while in medieval Europe magicians wore topaz rings in the belief that they could make the wearer invisible.

CHOOSING CRYSTALS

Choosing crystals is a very personal thing. For a start, you will perhaps prefer certain colors to others (see the exercise on stones and colors on page 24). You may be drawn to certain shapes, or even the touch, the size, or just the name. We all resonate to qualities; sometimes these are blueprints of symbols arising from deep within our unconscious.

When you pick out a crystal in a store, the chances are that the crystal has picked you out too. It is saying something to you, it is a living stone and its deepest nature is calling to you because you may lack that quality, or desire that quality in yourself. As soon as you choose the crystal, it will become an integral part of your life, so always thank it for being there and finding you too.

Sourcing crystals is quite easy these days, thanks to the Internet. Although you can buy them directly online, personally I always go to a specialist store or a mind/body/spirit or healing fair, where I can touch, see, and hold the crystals in my hand.

When selecting a crystal to buy, hold each crystal in your hand, even for as long as thirty seconds, until you know it's the right one for you. Sometimes you will feel a vibrational energy, or have an intuitive flash. This is a sign that you're in tune with the energy of the crystal and therefore the cosmos and its divine power.

After you have chosen your crystal and it is in your possession, repeat the following:

> *"Crystal of [say type of crystal], thank you for finding me."*

THE CORE TWELVE

For the purposes of this book, and as a beginner, the twelve standard crystals shown on the next page are an essential starter pack.

Choose one each of the twelve crystals shown below, which resonate to the twelve signs of the zodiac, thus bringing different qualities to life and giving you a good range of different energies. If you can't get hold of them, then you can always replace them with the other crystals associated with the planets and signs (see page 41). Purchase crystals that are all about the same size and shape, but it doesn't matter if they are polished or not.

There are many diverse lists of stones and crystals associated with the zodiac signs. Some say the crystal is associated with the month rather than the astrological zodiac, and these are often suggested in traditional sources, but here is my preferred list according to the symbol, color, and correspondences with astrological lore.

For good luck and to enhance your own sun-sign qualities, wear your crystal as jewelry or carry a piece in a pouch or bag. We will be looking in much more detail at astrological correspondences in Chapter Two.

THE CORE TWELVE CRYSTALS

RED CARNELIAN
(Aries)

EMERALD
(Taurus)

CITRINE
(Gemini)

MOONSTONE
(Cancer)

TIGER'S EYE
(Leo)

PERIDOT
(Virgo)

SAPPHIRE
(Libra)

OBSIDIAN
(Scorpio)

TURQUOISE
(Sagittarius)

GARNET
(Capricorn)

AMBER
(Aquarius)

AMETHYST
(Pisces)

CARING FOR CRYSTALS

If you choose to buy "tumbled stones," smaller pieces of crystal that have been turned for many hours in fine grit to give them a tough and smooth surface, they don't really need much care apart from a ritual cleansing after purchase. They can be kept in a pouch or bag as they rarely damage one another.

But many crystals are fragile, particularly those whose structure is layered or in clusters like the agates and white quartz crystals. These can easily splinter or crack, and any natural points or finely polished surfaces can scratch or chip.

Most crystals will need to be wrapped in a silk or cotton scarf or cloth to prevent scratching, and to protect against negativity, unless you are placing them in various points in the home. Always cleanse crystals after purchase, particularly jewelry, which may have been worn by someone else and may still carry their psychic footprints.

CLEANSING

When you first bring your crystals home, the first thing you should do is to cleanse them. Gently immersing them in the sea or under running stream water, or if you don't have access to either, under a running tap, is one simple method. As you do so, affirm in your mind or out loud that all negativity will be washed away, and positive energy will permeate the crystal.

You can also leave the crystal on a window ledge for three days and nights in a row to recharge its energy from both the sun's and moon's light.

Keep your polished or tumbled stones in a pouch or bag to guard against negative energy.

CLEANSING RITUAL

Another way to cleanse and re-energize a crystal is by this Fire, Earth, Air, and Water ritual. Once you have completed your set of twelve crystals, it can be performed on the whole set in one go. Its correspondence to the four elements of astrology brings extra symbolic power.

WHAT YOU WILL NEED:

- Your crystals
- A white candle
- A bowl of spring water
- A piece of paper and pen

1. Write down the names of your twelve crystals on the piece of paper and place the twelve crystals alongside their names (they can be in any order). This represents the element of Air, which is about "naming things." When we name things, we bring them to life in our own world.

2. Now gaze at the crystals on your paper and imagine them surrounded by golden light from the core of the Earth, cleansing, energizing, and nurturing them. As you gaze at them, "name" them one by one, either saying their names aloud or in your mind.

3. Now light the candle and take each crystal in turn and pass it slowly (being careful not to burn yourself!) through the top of the candle flame. By doing this you are cleansing and energizing the crystal by Fire.

4. Next, place the crystals on the table in a circle to symbolize Earth. Touch each crystal in turn with a drop of water from the bowl on your finger. As you do so, say the following for each crystal:

"With this Water from this Earth you are now cleansed and purified."

Finally, thank the crystals for being there for you, and then blow out the candle. Your crystals are now ready to be dedicated and, if desired, programmed.

DEDICATING A CRYSTAL

Once you have your crystal in your possession, you need to dedicate it, with the intention that only positive energy will flow through it, and it is only going to be used for the good of all. This dedication will focus all the goodness of the Universe into the crystal, and also purges any negative energy that may have already been attached to the stone, whether from it being handled by others, or from any geopathic stress that permeated the crystal during its formation deep within the Earth's surface.

Although crystals absorb and neutralize negative energy, turning it into positive energy, these outside influences can become ghostly hangers-on if the stone hasn't been used or treated with love or care for some time. Often stones hang around in shops or are in transit and don't take kindly to being treated like poor cattle on their way to market! So it's important to dedicate your crystals to positive healing energies to protect them from any other negative influences in the future too.

Look after your crystals as you would your most treasured friends.

DEDICATION RITUAL

When dedicating your crystals to positive healing energy, you will find that you begin to feel an affinity for the stone in question. Always make sure that you use the crystal only for the power of goodness and not to cause bad influences on anyone, including yourself.

1. Sit down in a quiet place with the crystal cupped in your hands. Close your eyes and focus on your breathing, taking deep, slow, regular breaths. Make sure your feet are both flat on the floor, preferably without shoes, so that you are grounded and feel a connection to the Earth.

2. In your mind, imagine you are like a tree, rooted to the ground, and from your feet a golden light begins to rise up through you, until its warmth fills every cell of your body. As it spreads throughout you it then enters the crystal, filling it with harmony and heat from the very depths of the Earth.

3. Now visualize a ray of pure white light beaming down from above, as if it has come from the galaxies and the Universe. As this light envelops you it merges with the golden warmth so you and the crystal are both protected, nurtured, and filled with positive energy.

4. Next, say this dedication either aloud or in your mind:

> *"This crystal will only be used for the highest good."*

5. Now open your eyes and gaze at your stone while repeating the dedication to the crystal five times and ending with the words, "So mote it be."

You can also dedicate your stone to a specific entity who protects and guides you, such as a deity, saint, guardian angel, or spirit guide. Once you have completed your dedication, you will find yourself more in tune with your crystal's powers. You are now ready to program it.

PROGRAMMING YOUR CRYSTALS

Crystals can be programmed so that their energy is focused on something specific and so that your intention is reinforced by the crystal's own power. Once a stone has been programmed, it will continually work with that desire until it is cleared or reprogrammed.

Although one crystal can convey, say, two or three intentions at the same time, it's important that they are compatible. In other words, if you seek new romance, but also wish to forget a past love affair, it would be wise to use two different crystals for these two very different desires!

Of course, you can just program your crystals for general themes such as for healing, protection, or spiritual guidance. You might wish for more love or prosperity, or to improve your home or work environment.

Each crystal can be charged with specific energy and is best used for just one intention.

PROGRAMMING RITUAL

Before programming your crystals, write down a list of what you want to manifest or change in your life. When you come to practice the ritual you will find it's easier to select specific stones.

1. Make sure you know exactly what your best intentions for the crystal are. Be specific and precise with your thoughts or words. If you want to find a new career or job, then describe exactly what kind of work you are seeking.

2. Select a stone that resonates to the desire. Make sure it is exactly the right crystal for your purpose. For example, if you are looking for peace and calm, choose a crystal that is already used as a meditational aid, such as selenite. If you want to stimulate action or to bring positive results quickly, select an energizing red stone, such as red carnelian, garnet, or ruby. For better communication choose a yellow stone, such as citrine.

3. Sit quietly with the crystal in the palm of your hand, and think about your desire. Keep repeating this desire or intention over and over, aloud or in your head.

4. Gaze at the crystal and relax as you feel the energy of the crystal in harmony with you. Now repeat your desire several times out loud to fix it to the crystal. You will intuitively feel when the programming is complete.

Once a stone has been programmed, depending on its purpose, wear the stone, carry it in your pocket, or place it by your bed. It can also be beneficial to hold the crystal and repeat your intentions several times a day too.

Keep any specifically programmed crystals out of contact with others, to avoid them being contacted by other energies and vibrations that may disturb your own program. Protect the crystal by wrapping it in silk or cotton when not in use.

If you decide you don't need the desire, or it has been fulfilled, to de-program the crystal simply sit comfortably with the crystal in your hand and say:

> *"All that I desired is no longer my intention; crystal, be as you once were."*

THE CRYSTAL COLOR PALETTE

We all have our favorite crystals, or we can use specific crystals to enhance our best qualities. However, there are some crystal colors that you can't be without. A bit like a painter who has a select number of colors on his palette, if you choose maybe one from each of the following colors to work with, the ones that "feel" right to you, or speak to you in some way, they will add another dimension to your collection.

According to quantum physics, everything in the Universe contains vibrational energy, whether the cells of your body, or the rippling water of a lake. These vibrational waves make up the electromagnetic spectrum. This spectrum includes radio waves, infrared, ultraviolet and visible light, X-rays, and gamma rays. In the visible part of the spectrum, the colors we humans can see range from the low frequency vibration of red, to the shortest wavelength and highest frequency, ultraviolet. The electromagnetic vibration of crystal energy also corresponds to this color spectrum.

Knowing what basic colors mean and the energy they invoke in your life means you can quickly grasp the basics of crystal power. The general rule is that if a color makes you feel good about yourself, by carrying or wearing a crystal corresponding to that color, those qualities will be enhanced.

YOUR COLOR PALETTE

1. Think about the colors you like most in your life right now. Do you prefer strong vivid reds, lively yellows, or passionate purple? Have you always painted your kitchen the same color, or do you change your color theme when it suits you?

2. Write down a list of colors you like, and a list of the colors you don't like. One list might be longer than the other, but it will show how you respond to color. If you find your "don't like" list is much longer, you may need to learn to be more objective about colors so that you can work with crystals more effectively.

BLUE CRYSTALS

In mystical traditions, the color blue has long been thought to enhance intuition, generate compassion, and invoke spiritual development. Blue crystals include those that edge towards violet and lavender blue, such as varieties of agate and tourmaline. As you will see from the sample selection, blue crystals all have a common theme, so it's easy to see how these crystals can work in your life.

SAPPHIRE:
• *wisdom* • *spiritual awareness*
• *prosperity*

BLUE LACE AGATE:
• *clarity* • *peace and serenity*

LAPIS LAZULI:
• *enlightenment*
• *reveals inner truths*

THE POWER OF BLUE

1. Take a blue crystal in your hand. It doesn't have to be one shown here; any blue crystal will enable you to experience the power of "blue."

2. Now gently release your grip on the crystal and let it lie in the palm of your hand again for a few minutes. It may feel cooler, warmer, different—whatever change you notice is important as it means you are beginning to connect to its power.

3. Next, repeat this affirmation to welcome the crystal as your friend:

> *"Your powers will help and guide me to listen to my own intuition and to understand I am part of the universal oneness. Thank you for your patience."*

4. Now place the crystal under your pillow. Within one lunar cycle (about a month) you will have significantly developed your psychic awareness.

AQUAMARINE:
• *opens intuition* • *invokes tolerance and calms the mind*

AZURITE:
• *invokes soul awareness*
• *spiritual vision*

BLUE TOPAZ:
• *brings trust in the universe*
• *attainment of goals*

RED CRYSTALS

Red is the color of fire, passion, growth, impulse, power, action, courage, and love. It also signifies blood, the life force and energy that gets us moving. Red empowers, uplifts, and gets things done. It's all about action and drive; so, for example, if you are suffering from a lack of power, you may need a red crystal in your life. Red crystals include the bloodstone, with its spots of blood-like red (hence its name), intense red garnet and red carnelian, and the cooler red ruby.

BLOODSTONE:
• courage • determination
• personal power

RUBY:
• passion • vitality • sexuality

GARNET:
• strength • willpower • charisma

RED CARNELIAN:
• adventure • motivation
• endurance

RED TIGER'S EYE:
• leadership • authority • action

RED JASPER:
• quick-thinking
• confidence • results

FILL YOURSELF WITH COURAGE

1. Take a red crystal from your storehouse of crystals. Any red crystal will do as it is the color red you are going to invoke in your life.

2. Close your eyes and hold the stone between both palms of your hands, as if clasping them together in prayer. Imagine the stone slowly warming up in your hand, bringing you its inner fire to light your own. Imagine this warmth spreading through your body, circulating throughout you from your toes to the top of your head. As you are filled with "fire," think of one thing you want to do in the next week, something you've never done before, and thought you were incapable of doing. Imagine yourself now doing it. Reflect on this image of you doing the very thing you have not yet achieved and imagine the great results achieved.

3. Once you come out of your visualization, place the red crystal in a safe place and remind yourself that the following week you will do exactly what you had imagined, now that the color red has filled you with courage.

YELLOW/ORANGE CRYSTALS

Yellow is thought to be the color of communication, wisdom, joy, and happiness. It is also the color that brings clarity and a sharp mind. When yellow moves into orange, the qualities of red's warmth and mindfulness are included. Orange-yellow imparts a sense of focus, while the clean light yellow of fluorite clears the mind, making it active and alert. Use yellow or orange stones for clarity, decision-making, sharper memory, and concentration skills.

YELLOW TOPAZ:
• *clarity* • *decision-making*
• *well-being*

AMBER:
• *joyful* • *carefree* • *vitalizing*

CITRINE:
• *imagination* • *manifestation*
• *creative thinking*

YELLOW FLUORITE:
• *alertness* • *sharpens memory*

ORANGE OR
YELLOW CALCITE:
• *concentration* • *intellectual power*

STIRRING THE IMAGINATION

You will need a pen and paper for this exercise. Take any yellow or orange stone in your writing hand and gently close your fist around it. Close your eyes and concentrate for a moment on the color yellow. Repeat over and over in your head the word "focus" as you feel the power of the crystal generate clarity and creativity. After two minutes or so, unclench your fist, remove the stone, and start writing down a list of all the goals or dreams you have for the future. These will come quickly to you now you have been energized by the crystal. When you have finished repeat the following:

"Thank you [say type of crystal] for stirring my imagination so that I can now manifest a dream."

GREEN CRYSTALS

Green is the color of self-respect, well-being, and balance. It also symbolizes learning, growth, and harmony, and it is a powerful healer for vitalizing the life force. On another level, green can promote material and financial success. Green jade is a sacred stone in parts of eastern Asia, used in feng shui to promote successful business. All green crystals have the power to invoke growth, to welcome change, to pursue new ideas, or to free yourself from the demands of others.

MALACHITE:
• transformation • abundance • exploration

GREEN TOURMALINE:
• money and success attractor

JADE:
• financial creativity • decision-making

EMERALD:
• wisdom • foresight • inspiration

PERIDOT:
• clarity • self-acceptance • responsibility

GREEN AVENTURINE:
• insight • leadership • prosperity

THE ENERGY OF GREEN

Take a green crystal and hold it between the palms of your hands. Imagine all the money in the world coming your way, millions and millions flowing through the power of the crystal into your hands. Then imagine it all flowing away again as you slowly open your hands to let the crystal lie gently in one palm. Open your eyes and reflect upon how much there is out there that can be manifested through the energy of green and this green stone. In the future the Universe will give you how much you want, as long as you give out the same amount of love and compassion too.

BLACK/BROWN CRYSTALS

Although black is not technically a color because it absorbs all light, it is still an important "energy" in the crystal kingdom. It is an energy of emptiness into which anything may emerge and disappear once again, providing a sense of potential and possibility in the future. Black gemstones have often been used as stones of prophecy. On another level, they symbolize self-control and resilience. Brown aligns to the color of earth and is associated with the material or down-to-earth side of life, connecting us to stability and encouraging acceptance of the tangible world.

BLACK TOURMALINE:
• *protective* • *grounding*
• *rational thinking*

ONYX:
• *strength* • *self-control*
• *future potential*

JET:
• *stability* • *protection*
• *balance*

MAHOGANY OBSIDIAN:
• *purpose* • *self-awareness*
• *self-belief*

BRONZITE:
• *self-confidence* • *discernment*
• *inspiration*

MAGNETITE:
• *tenacity* • *endurance*
• *objectivity*

THE LIGHT OF YOURSELF

This exercise will help you to understand how black can be the energy that reveals your inner light. Light a candle and place a brown/black crystal on the table in front of you.

1. Concentrate for a while on the stone, visualizing yourself entering the deeper matrix of the stone's very being, into the darkness, and within that dark center finding a light.

2. As you "walk" through the eternal light within the dark, imagine you are now invisible, invincible, understanding the unknown as much as you do the known.

3. Stop for a while and be aware of a restful silence, an emptiness within and a connection to the power of the Universe as it envelops you with purpose, balance, and self-esteem.

4. Slowly let the visualization go from your mind, touch the stone with all your fingers of both hands, and then gently move them away from the stone to release you from the energy.

WHITE/CLEAR/PINK CRYSTALS

White crystals (or clear crystals that have no color) are symbolic of new beginnings and development in any direction. White clears clutter and obstacles away, brings mental and spiritual clarity, and purifies thoughts and actions so you can see how to be truly fortunate. Pink crystals invoke feelings of caring, tenderness, self-worth, love, and acceptance.

MOONSTONE:
• *psychic awareness* • *healing*
• *new beginnings*

CLEAR QUARTZ:
• *balance* • *purity*
• *amplifies desire*

FINDING CLARITY

Take a clear crystal in one hand. Hold it tightly for a few minutes until you are aware of its vibrational energy. As you hold it, imagine you are filled with love for yourself and others, and complete awareness of who you are and where you are going. Look into the crystal as if it were a crystal ball. What can you see? Shapes? Strange formations, lines, cracks, mysterious ancient pathways that this crystal has experienced in its geological time span? Imagine how this cosmic energy is working through the crystal and into your hand, and as you look, how the clarity of the color white, which has all the colors of the electromagnetic spectrum contained within it, is within you too. Close your eyes as you untighten your grasp on your crystal, and thank it for its powerful link to the Universe.

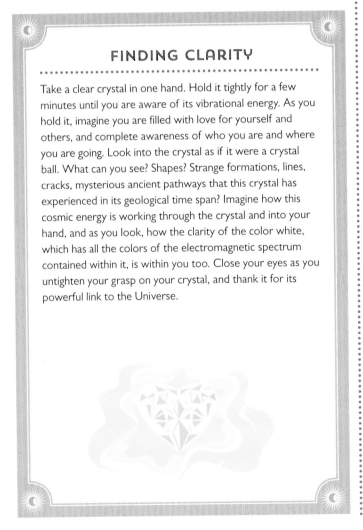

WHITE SELENITE:
• *insight* • *foresight*
• *reconciliation* • *peace*

SILVER OR WHITE TOPAZ:
• *cosmic awareness*
• *clarity* • *truth*

ROSE QUARTZ:
• *harmony* • *love*
• *peace* • *romance*

RHODOCHROSITE:
• *self-worth* • *compassion*
• *acceptance*

PURPLE/VIOLET CRYSTALS

Purple has been used to symbolize magic, mystery, and spirituality, and was once a color favored by royalty. A mixture of red (dynamic and active energy) and blue (otherworldly and intuitive), purple is a color of creativity, imagination, inspiration, and universal wisdom.

AMETHYST:
• *tranquility* • *spiritual wisdom*
• *intuition*

PURPLE SAPPHIRE:
• *oneness* • *psychic vision*
• *awakening*

PURPLE FLUORITE:
• *meditation*
• *psychic communication*

SUGILITE:
• *spiritual love* • *self-understanding*
• *revelation*

CHAROITE:
• *transformation* • *unconditional love*
• *clarity*

THE PURPLE BUBBLE

Choose a purple crystal and place it on the palm of one hand. Close your eyes and imagine the color purple as a huge bubble above your head. Keep holding the vision of the purple bubble as it moves down slowly to surround you so that you are inside the bubble with the crystal. Visualize the purple filling you with a sense of universal connection and a feeling of utter peace, just as the crystal is doing to you now. Now let the bubble gradually fade away in your mind. When it has gone, open your eyes to see your crystal reflecting that purple spirituality before you. Make an affirmation to the crystal: "Thank you for bringing me the light of the Universe"; then place it under your pillow for one lunar cycle (about a month) to activate your own spiritual awareness.

THE USES OF CRYSTALS

Before you begin to work with crystals, it is important to know how you can use them for the different forms of healing, divination, and protective influences referred to in this book. When you come to work with the key exercises in specific chapters, you will then be aware of what power or energies you are invoking—and so will your crystal!

PROTECTION

You can use a whole range of crystals to make you feel safe or protected in your daily life, whether that be when traveling to ensure a safe trip, to guard against bad business, or to ward off negativity from external and internal influences.

So, exactly what kind of protection do you need, and why are you seeking help? Try asking yourself the following questions:

TIGER'S EYE:
• *focus* • *opportunity*

1. NEGATIVE INFLUENCE

Is there a negative influence that can bring harm to your home, family, business, personal sense of security, happiness, or quality of life?

Once you have identified what this negative influence is, place a crystal near the main entrance to your home to promote positive energy. For example, use tiger's eye for focus and opportunity, or citrine for abundance. You can, of course, also use crystals such as obsidian to absorb negative energy. But the key to self-protection is to find the source of the negativity and, rather than merely guard and surround yourself with a crystal "moat" or fortress, fill your world with beneficial crystal energy. This energy will restore balance and harmony around you, which in itself spills over into the world beyond your "moat."

CITRINE:
• *abundance*

OBSIDIAN:
• *absorbs negative energy*

2. NEGATIVE SELF

Are you negative yourself? Some of us are our own worst enemy. We cannot let go of our personal fears, or we believe we need to be protected from being hurt by others. We obsess about what is done to us, rather than what we can do to look at life from a positive angle. Our priorities are upside down, and in fact we need protection from our own self-sabotage. If you suspect you are a negative person, there are crystals that can balance and bring you back to a positive sense of yourself, protecting you from your own inner demons. For example, chrysoberyl will boost your sense of self-worth, while blue tourmaline prevents negative thoughts from taking over your mind.

3. THREAT TO HAPPINESS

Is there someone or something who poses a threat to your happiness? Does a particular person or environment leave you feeling depressed or unhappy?

One of the best all-round crystals for decluttering negative minds and atmospheres is fluorite; this can be your first port of call for any kind of protection you need.

4. FEAR AND ANXIETY

Are you fearful watching the news? Do you suffer anxiety about everything?

If so, you are probably out of harmony with yourself and your environment. Things are out of balance when you see only the dark side of life. Amazonite is the supreme harmony stone. It expands your ability to see multiple points of view on any situation and enhances a positive viewpoint on your life and the world. Lepidolite is a natural sedative stone, bringing calm and a positive outlook on life.

FLUORITE:
• *decluttering negative minds and atmospheres*

BLUE TOURMALINE:
• *blocks negative thoughts*

AMAZONITE:
• *harmony*

CRYSTAL HEALING

From the protective attributes of crystals, we move on to healing crystals. To deal with any medical condition of the body, you need to be properly trained or work with someone properly qualified. Although crystals are often used in medical practices, and have been used to treat many diseases throughout history, we are only going to concentrate in this book on the key crystals used for emotional healing, life enhancement, and for balancing chakras—the important invisible energy centers located throughout the body that are the emanations of our spiritual self.

Crystal healing works via the vibrational resonance and balancing of the chakras. The chakras are invisible spirals of energy that flow through and around the body. Via the chakras we are connected to the Universe itself. Crystals are also used to balance environmental influences, such as geopathic stress, where there is unwanted negative energy in the Earth, landscape, or home. This may include spiritual disturbances, such as negativity left by past occupants or left over from a bad love relationship.

ᛏ Crystals can be placed on the body to aid in healing emotional and physical problems (the latter is best left to the skilled practitioner).

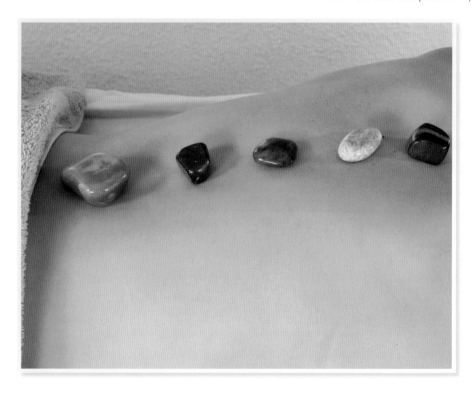

For example, placing malachite in the southeast corner of your home will encourage money problems to disappear, but also brings abundance in other ways. It works on a deeper level to heal the soul, and its spiritual disconnection. Your money worries are rooted in the fact that you are so bound up in the trappings of materialism that you have disconnected from the Universe. Other crystals such as citrine will help you to reconnect to the cosmos. It is this kind of holistic healing that takes place on various levels.

Using a dowsing pendulum can help you to find lost objects or make important decisions for the future.

DIVINATION

Crystals have been used for divination too, and their vibrational power is linked to that of the cosmos. This means they can be used as a conduit or channel for deeper knowledge and access to the universal storehouse of knowledge from which all future, past, and present information comes to us. As a divinatory tool, they are usually associated with astrological symbols, the zodiac, and corresponding planetary forces.

There are various crystals that correspond to the twelve signs of the zodiac, and each crystal vibrates to the astrological resonance of the planets and the signs (see page 41).

Zodiac crystals can be laid out in a spread in a way similar to tarot cards and runes. Alternatively, one can be picked from a pouch or bag as your crystal guide or oracle for the day. Events and encounters throughout the day will align with the symbolic language of the crystal and empower you with its specific qualities.

For example, say you randomly picked blue lace agate (see page 50), the chances are you will experience a flash of insight or perfect vision of your future goals during that day.

THE AMAZING POWER OF CRYSTALS

Wearing jewelry and placing crystals in certain environments can transform, enhance, and harmonize the local energy and its surroundings. You may choose green tourmaline to boost your confidence, or amber to absorb negative energy. To attract love, place rose quartz, or for abundance a piece of tiger's eye.

Crystals can protect you from other people's negativity, such as smoky quartz and amethyst. To attract others, or just to attract good fortune, place citrine and unpolished emerald in your home; wear the banded pink rhodochrosite for new romance. But before you start to learn about crystal placement, healing, and divination, you need to first experience this amazing power for yourself.

If you remember, crystals are "living stones." In other words, they are not just inanimate objects, they are filled with their own unique energy. They must be treated with respect, just as you would treat a friend, and they will need to be dedicated and cleansed before you use them. So let's get to work, starting with an exercise designed to open you up to the vibrational energy of you, simply by invoking the power of a white quartz crystal.

Once you have chosen a selection of your favorite crystals, always remember that they are "living stones" and are as such your friends.

WHITE QUARTZ POWER

WHAT YOU WILL NEED:

- A white quartz crystal
- A table
- A white candle

1. Place a white candle on a table and a piece of white quartz crystal of hand-held size in front of the candle. Sit comfortably at the table and light your candle. Once the flame begins to still itself, take up the white quartz crystal and place it in one of your palms. Close your eyes, and breathe slowly and gently, counting down your breaths from twenty to one, to settle yourself into a calming rhythm. As you let the crystal rest in your palm, notice first what it feels like in your hand. Is it cold, warm, soft, hard, heavy, light? Now, move it into the other hand and take note of what it makes you feel.

2. Next, open your eyes and see the crystal's shape and color, the light that may be refracted within its inner world. Imagine yourself exploring the innermost world of your white quartz crystal until you are reaching the pure light of the Universe. Now close your eyes again and reflect upon the energy, its vibrations, as you open yourself to its unique language. Can you sense it is alive? Can you hear what it is telling you?

3. Place the crystal back on the table and repeat the affirmation:

"I am blessed by the presence of this crystal, and I am empowered by the energy that flows through the Universe."

4. Take your time to come back to the "real world" by blowing out or snuffing the candle. Take a few deep breaths and then ground yourself by doing some ordinary chore in your daily life. You have now had your first experience of crystal power.

CHAPTER TWO

THE KEY to UNDERSTANDING & WORKING WITH CRYSTALS

 Get to know twenty-two of the most popular and useful crystals

....

 Astrology helps you to understand the stone's affinity

....

 Strengthen your psychic power to connect to the Universe

....

 Feng shui techniques to improve home and lifestyle

THE ZODIAC, PLANETS, AND CRYSTALS

We've looked at how crystals of the same color resonate to similar qualities or energies, and we'll be using many of them in the forthcoming pages. But first we're going to learn how the cosmic energy is showcased through the planets.

Since ancient times, crystals have been believed to embody the different energies of the planets and fixed stars via their vibrations. Symbolically, the planets still have a powerful significance for us through the art of astrology, and their correspondences in astrology resonate to your zodiac sign and its associated stone. As mentioned before, you can wear your own zodiac sign crystal or carry it with you to promote your best qualities, but your planetary stone is like a "power stone" and will enhance all aspects of your life. If you take it with you or wear it wherever you go, its influence will help you to experience the best of yourself in life and to feel at one with the Universe.

Whatever your zodiac sign, every crystal will complement you with its specific energy, at any time you need to boost this quality in your life. For example, if you're a Capricorn, a garnet would maximize your ambitious business plan. If you also wore or carried a moonstone, you would be able to intuit other people's real motives in your business dealings.

There are ten planet crystals (the Earth isn't included in traditional Western astrology) and twelve zodiac crystals, making a total of twenty-two crystals, which also correspond to the twenty-two Major Arcana cards of the tarot. As you will see in Chapter Three, you can also program your crystals with tarot energy to manifest the things you want in your life.

The exercises here all use the specific crystal in the text, but if you can't get hold of it, either replace with a similar crystal from the color section in Chapter One, or simply perform the exercise while "visualizing" the specific crystal in your hand or where it is intended to be placed. Imagination is a powerful part of the mind that links us directly to the supernatural forces of the Universe, so imagining your crystal ritual will invoke a similar magic by association to the crystal's power itself.

TABLE OF PLANETS/SIGNS AND CRYSTALS

SIGN OR PLANET	SYMBOL	CRYSTAL	KEYWORD
The Sun	☉	Topaz	Charisma
The Moon	☽	Selenite	Intuition
Mercury	☿	Agate	Logic
Venus	♀	Tourmaline	Attraction
Mars	♂	Bloodstone	Courage
Jupiter	♃	Lapis lazuli	Enlightenment
Saturn	♄	Onyx	Integrity
Uranus	♅	Aquamarine	Self-expression
Neptune	♆	Blue lace agate	Creativity
Pluto	♇	Malachite	Wealth
Aries	♈	Ruby	Passionate
Taurus	♉	Emerald	Practical
Gemini	♊	Citrine	Versatile
Cancer	♋	Moonstone	Sensitive
Leo	♌	Tiger's eye	Radiant
Virgo	♍	Peridot	Discriminating
Libra	♎	Blue sapphire	Diplomatic
Scorpio	♏	Obsidian	Powerful
Sagittarius	♐	Turquoise	Adventurous
Capricorn	♑	Garnet	Ambitious
Aquarius	♒	Amber	Original
Pisces	♓	Amethyst	Visionary

THE PLANETS AND STONES

THE SUN
⊶ Rules Leo

The Sun is our nearest star, giving life on Earth, and around which all the other planets orbit. There have been sun deities throughout ancient history. Worshiping the sun as life-bringer and light-giver has been at the core of many civilizations and cultures. We still have "sun-worshipers" today—who laze around on beaches or lie on sunbeds. The sun symbolizes not only light but the new dawn, the outward expression of the Self, and one's ego. In ancient Egypt the sun was associated with the gods Horus (representing the rising sun), Osiris (the setting sun), and Ra (the sun's zenith).

GOLDEN TOPAZ
⊶ Regenerates and shines

Empowered with illuminating energy, golden topaz is the crystal of optimism, charisma, and self-confidence, and gives you, its friend, the ability to shine. It helps to shed light on what your inner riches are. When you wear it or carry it with you, you can be sure that your own inner radiance will be attracting all the right attention, spreading happiness all around.

For fame and fortune, this stone bestows you with its power to strengthen your own resources, but also to have a little help from the cosmos. It attracts mentors, the ability to be in the right place at the right time, and chance moments when good fortune will be in your favor.

BE A SUN DEITY

Hold a piece of golden topaz in your hand and imagine you are a sun deity. You appear from the east in the morning to ride your golden chariot across the sky. You know you must flee to the west to avoid the dark of the nighttime gods, and yet you know that come the morning, you will shine again. This simple visualization technique will align you to the power of topaz.

THE MOON

⚷ Rules Cancer

If the sun is the life-bringer, the moon has always been associated with the darkness and nighttime. Similarly, the moon is about all things feminine, receiving and giving, passive and intuitive, comforting and belonging. In ancient Greek mythology, Selene, the sister of the sun god Helios, was the personification of the moon itself. The moon goddess is renowned for her passionate love affair with the beautiful mortal Edymion, upon whom she cast a spell of eternal sleep so that he remained forever deathless and ageless, and so that she could make love to him in his sleep.

SELENITE

⚷ Bridges the spiritual and earthly realms

Named after the moon goddess, translucent or pure white selenite has a fine vibration and instills peace, intuition, and telepathic power. The stone clears confusion and promotes clarity and the ability to see the other side of the coin, or the dark side of the moon itself. It also enables you to be aware of what occurs at an unconscious level. Selenite maximizes your intuition and psychic awareness and can help

you to access universal truth. It is a powerful tool for scrying—looking into its depths to divine the future and to learn about the past. It is a truth stone, opening you up to higher planes of consciousness.

ALIGNING TO THE MOON

Place a piece of selenite on a window ledge during the full moon. The following day keep it with you and see how it invokes peace, serenity, and intuitive problem-solving. Hold it in your hand for a few minutes at the end of the day and reflect on how you resonate to the power of this highly spiritual stone.

MERCURY

o—┐ Rules Gemini and Virgo

Personified as the messenger of the gods, Mercury is the closest planet to the Sun. Its astrological influence is about sharp wits, communication on any level, and the ability to rationalize and be logical. However, the god Mercury, originally Hermes in Greek mythology, was also a trickster, the god of thieves, tradesmen, and deception. When Mercury influences our lives, on one level we are unreliable, but on another we can perfect the art of persuasion. We can also be intellectually cunning and use quick wits to move on from a difficult situation.

NATURAL AGATE

o—┐ The crystal of realistic intelligence

This banded crystal appears in a variety of colors. For the best alignment to Mercurial power choose milky white with shades of brown or cream. Through its multiple layers it reveals different layers of meaning, bringing its Mercurial energy to life. Natural agate improves concentration and overcomes emotional negativity, enhancing objectivity and intellectual strength. Agate bestows you with self-analytical ability and encourages a logical, realistic frame of mind. It dispels anger or tension, creating self-confidence and the desire to "say your piece."

BANISH NEGATIVE THINKING

With a piece of agate resting in the palm of your hand, repeat the following blessing:

"Lover of truth, worker of logic, I am graced with down-to-earth intelligence. Let it be so."

Take time to sense its vibrational influence in your hand, then write down a list of your positive qualities while the stone helps to banish negative thinking from your mind.

VENUS

○━┓ **Rules Taurus and Libra**

This astrological planet of love, seduction, romance, and pleasure was once thought by ancient civilizations to be two different heavenly bodies, the Morning Star and the Evening Star. And it is this dual perception of Venus (albeit now only symbolic) that reveals her dual nature as love-bringer, but also as jealous intruder. In Greek mythology, she was known as Aphrodite. Jealous of the other goddesses' claim to beauty, she tricked Paris into falling in love with Helen of Troy, which resulted in the Trojan War.

PINK TOURMALINE

○━┓ **The stone of romantic attraction**

Pink tourmaline cleanses and purifies, but it also attracts love to you in both the physical and spiritual sense. It helps you to love yourself, first and foremost, and inspires others to love you too. The crystal bestows you with harmonious feelings, enriches your sex life, and promotes compassion and true love. If you carry or wear pink tourmaline, you will attract new romance, others will warm to you, and all aspects of love will be favorable. Any negativity is dispelled, as the heart chakra is cleansed to bring you serenity and romantic energy.

SENSING OTHERS

Wear or carry pink tourmaline for one day and note the effect you have on others or that they have on you. Ask the following questions to aid you:

- *Do you feel it enhances your seductive powers?*

- *Do you feel kinder towards others?*

- *Have you fallen in love with someone?*

- *What does it mean to be empowered with love?*

MARS
○—┐ Rules Aries

Feisty, self-centered, and impulsive energy is represented in astrology by the planet Mars. Personified as the Roman god of war, and known as the "red planet," Mars is also associated with masculine energies, with courage, battles, risk, motivation, and determination. Although his Greek predecessor, the god Ares, was viewed primarily as a destructive force by the Romans, Mars represented military power as a way to secure peace. Mars was no longer a wild, untamed, destabilizing god; he had been civilized.

BLOODSTONE
○—┐ The stone of courage and valor

If Mars is about potency and new blood, then the bloodstone, with its spots of red, revitalizes the mind and spirit. Also known as heliotrope, this stone was once thought to banish evil, to help the wearer avoid dangerous situations, and even to control the weather. Bloodstone gives you the courage to face new challenges. It also helps you to deal with new or unexpected circumstances, so that instead of fearing sudden change, you "go with the flow." Wearing or carrying bloodstone will help you to make crucial decisions and to trust your instincts.

LEARNING COURAGE

Hold your bloodstone in your hand for about five minutes to connect to your own courage and initiative. Then, place it in your pocket or pouch and intentionally go and do something you wouldn't normally do. For example, eat some form of food you have never tried; ask a seemingly uninterested object of your affection out for a date; if you only usually go to see comedies, go to see a weepy film. You will be amazed at your courage.

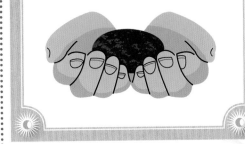

4

JUPITER

⚬⟶ Rules Sagittarius

This planet symbolizes exploration, excess, bounty, and passion, and, with many of the planet's moons named after Jupiter's various lovers, it also signifies "big love." The Roman god Jupiter was the king of the heavens; his Greek counterpart, Zeus, was highly promiscuous. Zeus went around heaven and earth sweeping nymphs and mortals off their feet. This energy is about grand schemes, grand potential, grand belief, and grand promise of more to come. Optimistic and seductive, Jupiter's crystals are there to uplift and invoke abundance.

LAPIS LAZULI

⚬⟶ The stone of wisdom and fame

Its deep blue color, often flecked with gold, is unmistakable. Renowned for its use as a cosmetic in ancient Egyptian times and later as a pigment prized by Renaissance painters, the crystal enhances all forms of knowledge, wisdom, and learning. Like Jupiter, it gives "big" thoughts, great self-expression, and yet, at a deeper level, spiritual understanding. Like the god Jupiter, lapis lazuli is prolific, enlightening, and can help you to study, to love, to find meaning in life, or simply

to express yourself as an individual. Wear or carry lapis lazuli in the workplace to attract promotion or success in your field.

SHOWING OFF

Close your eyes and imagine that you want to be a star. Imagine you stand before the biggest audience you have ever seen. You are singing, playing a musical instrument, or performing on the stage. Now imagine a piece of lapis lazuli hanging around your neck. As you begin your performance, you feel it touching your skin, dissolving all fear, enhancing your talents. If you are truly looking for fame, practice this visualization with a piece of lapis lazuli held in your hand every day, and your chance for the limelight will follow suit.

SATURN

○━ Rules Capricorn

In medieval astrology, Saturn was considered the planet of melancholy and loneliness. Yet it was through the qualities of self-absorption and introversion that magicians, philosophers, and artists fused with the universe, and so alchemy, science, art, and literature were born. Saturn is both a strict teacher and a reliable midwife. The planet's energy is concerned with self-control, awareness of limitations, mastery of skills, and inner and outer confidence. Saturn, known as Cronos in Greek mythology, overthrew his father Ouranus and ruled a 'Golden Age' of order, law, abundance, and opportunity. Crystals associated with this planet will therefore encourage order, integrity, serious thinking, and mastery in all you do.

ONYX

○━ The stone of self-mastery

This superb, usually marble-like black or burnt umber colored stone is considered to be the stone of self-mastery. It brings stability and wise decision-making to the wearer. It's also said that onyx contains the memories of all that happens to you while you wear it, and is as such a secret container for your life story. Onyx also enhances stamina and protects the wearer from negativity.

BEING SELF-RELIANT

Hold your stone in your hand and whisper to it one secret that you would never tell anyone else. Say it over three times, then place the onyx on a window ledge for one night of a full moon. The following day, take the onyx and hold it gently between your hands and allow its vibrational energy to merge with yours, knowing your secret is safe.

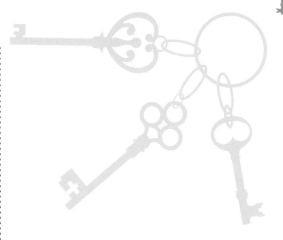

URANUS

o—⚹ Rules Aquarius

In Greek mythology, Ouranus, the god of the heavens, was castrated by his son, Cronus. The sky god's genitalia fell into the ocean, causing a mass of foam, from which Aphrodite, or Venus, was born. This planet, named after the sky god, is said in astrology to have a liberating but disruptive influence. In fact, Uranus upsets, shakes up, and disorganizes our lives to create progress. Similarly, Uranian crystals wake us up to who we really are, and can give us belief in our ideals and visions.

AQUAMARINE

o—⚹ The stone of progress

Known for its delicate blue-green color, Aquamarine inspires belief, truth, and trust in others and also in one's own judgment. It clears the way for progress and can enhance your ability to know what will be right for you in the future without having to make compromises. Like Uranus, whose genitalia gave birth to Venus, aquamarine also activates Venus-associated principles such as the ideals of love, beauty, and creative self-expression. Aquamarine wakes you up to who you really are and reveals your true path for the future.

KNOWING YOUR TRUE PATH

Take your piece of aquamarine and sit quietly with your eyes closed for several minutes. As you do so, imagine it taking you into the future, across the heavens and the oceans, and far into the distant galaxies. There you discover what you most desire for the future, the truth plain and simple. Let the crystal absorb these ideals as you come back to earth in your mind. Open your eyes and look into the aquamarine stone, and you will see it has changed color just by taking you into another plane of existence—your future one. Care for this stone well, and it will be your best friend.

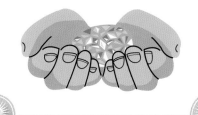

NEPTUNE

०—★ Rules Pisces

Discovered in the nineteenth century, this far-away planet in our solar system is battered by high speed winds and terrifying storms, such as the Great Dark Spot recorded in 1989, which lasted about five years. One of its moons, Triton, named after Greek god Neptune and Amphitrite's son, is a frozen world, thought to be the coldest realm in the solar system. In astrology, Neptune is considered to be a planet of creative inspiration, spiritual enlightenment, and romantic idealism, but it is also the planet of illusion, deception, loss, addiction, and dissolution.

BLUE LACE AGATE

०—★ The stone of visualization

To promote Neptune's beneficial attributes, such as accessing higher planes of consciousness, heightened intuition, and artistic inspiration, blue lace agate has a stimulating influence on moods and feelings. The soft, elegant colors of the stone reflect its ability to encourage, to support, and to accept one's vulnerable side. It enhances creative visualization, neutralizing stress, anger, and fear.

DISPELLING FEAR

Place the stone on a piece of paper, then draw circles or ovals around the stone to represent the storms of Neptune. Make a dot or tiny circle just outside the big circle to represent the moon Triton. Now concentrate on the stone, and imagine it calming the eternal storms, dissolving all that falls onto the planet, restoring beauty, and bringing serenity and peace. Take the stone and place it over Triton. Leaving your hands touching the stone, feel how the crystal is warming, melting the ice, and awakening the moon from its frozen state. This is how the stone will work with you too.

PLUTO
⚬—➤ Rules Scorpio

Now considered in astronomical terms to be a dwarf planet, Pluto is still known as the ninth planet of astrology and in terms of symbolism, is associated with the attributes of the Greek god of the Underworld and Earth's riches, Pluto (originally Hades). Pluto is about personal power, the dark side of life, taboo subjects, death, sex, and money. It is also about mystery, intensity, self-transformation, rebirth, regeneration, and destruction.

MALACHITE
⚬—➤ The stone of transformation

To harness the positive power of Pluto, malachite is the power stone that not only absorbs negative energy, but also promotes risk-taking, adventure, change, and self-transformation. Placed in the southeast corner of your home, it can encourage wealth and prosperity. Wearing the stone helps to keep new ventures or projects on schedule and life on track. The stones can be programmed to promote spiritual growth and commitment to a higher purpose, and they are often worn as talismans to invoke safety in travel.

FEELING ALIVE

Wear a malachite ring or carry a piece of malachite for the day. Note how intense and alive it makes you feel, and how determined you are to succeed. Write down a list of your best qualities that evening, then place the ring or stone on the paper, and repeat:

With this stone
I will soon be blessed
By the elements of north, south,
east, and west.

With charisma bold
and projects new
With ready mind, soul,
and spirit true.

Now place the stone in the southeast corner of your home to maximize the power of its associated energy. Soon, all that you imagine achieving will be yours.

THE ZODIAC CRYSTALS

These crystals are the most popular ones to promote the positive characteristics of your sun-sign. If these qualities are lacking in your life, then it's important to wear or carry the relevant crystal with you to reinforce its positive powers.

These are some of the most readily available and most useful crystals to work with. This detailed guide will help you to benefit from their specific qualities, whatever sign you are. There's also an exercise to help you understand the quality of each energy and to introduce you to these crystals' unique powers. All the planets and signs are shown as a zodiac wheel on the page opposite.

BLOODSTONE
RUBY
(Aries)

AMETHYST
BLUE LACE AGATE
(Pisces)

AQUAMARINE
AMBER
(Aquarius)

GARNET
ONYX
(Capricorn)

TURQUOISE
LAPIS LAZULI
(Sagittarius)

MALACHITE
OBSIDIAN
(Scorpio)

PINK TOURMALINE
BLUE SAPPHIRE
(Libra)

PERIDOT
AGATE
(Virgo)

TIGERS EYE
TOPAZ
(Leo)

SELENITE
MOONSTONE
(Cancer)

CITRINE
AGATE
(Gemini)

EMERALD
PINK TOURMALINE
(Taurus)

THE ZODIAC CRYSTAL WHEEL

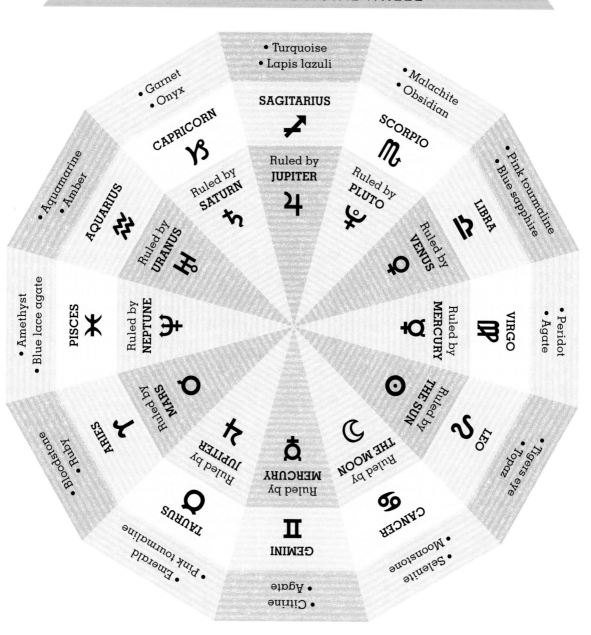

- Turquoise
- Lapis lazuli

SAGITARIUS

Ruled by **JUPITER**

- Malachite
- Obsidian

SCORPIO

Ruled by **PLUTO**

- Garnet
- Onyx

CAPRICORN

Ruled by **SATURN**

- Pink tourmaline
- Blue sapphire

LIBRA

Ruled by **VENUS**

- Aquamarine
- Amber

AQUARIUS

Ruled by **URANUS**

- Peridot
- Agate

VIRGO

Ruled by **MERCURY**

- Amethyst
- Blue lace agate

PISCES

Ruled by **NEPTUNE**

LEO

Ruled by **THE SUN**

- Tigers eye
- Topaz

- Bloodstone
- Ruby

ARIES

Ruled by **MARS**

THE MOON

Ruled by **CANCER**

- Selenite
- Moonstone

- Emerald
- Pink tourmaline

TAURUS

Ruled by **JUPITER**

Ruled by **MERCURY**

GEMINI

- Citrine
- Agate

ARIES
March 21—April 19

○━ **ZODIAC CRYSTAL:** Ruby

○━ **SYMBOL:** The Ram

○━ **ELEMENT:** Fire

Headstrong and goal-oriented, Aries are born to lead, with courage and passion for life and love. In love you are impatient, in work you get results, and at home you hope someone else will clear up after you. Your ability to take risks, stand out from the crowd, and show that you can win any battle leads you down challenging and adventurous pathways. With your competitive spirit, you are a force to be reckoned with and won't take "no" for an answer.

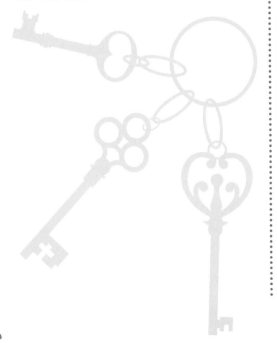

RUBY

In the medieval period, this stone of passion and fire was believed to have the power to boil water and melt wax. It was so prized by kings, emperors, and nobility that its value was greater than that of a diamond. It was also worn as an amulet to ward off plague and was thought to warn its wearer of impending danger, banish evil, restrain lust, and to help resolve disputes. In fact, its mythical powers extended to making the wearer totally invulnerable. Ruby is used to promote passion, sensuality, and deep, long-lasting love. It sharpens the mind, attracts others to you, and invokes enthusiasm and dynamism. Whenever you need to be energized, or fired into action, then wear or carry ruby wherever you go.

UNLEASHING YOUR DRIVE

Sit quietly with your eyes closed, holding your ruby, and imagine you have just met the lover of your dreams. Feel the ruby exuding lust, heat, power, desire, and fire into you. All this energy moves through every part of your body until you are ready for action. Stand up, open your eyes, and stare into the red of the ruby and you will see the passion of this iconic stone.

TAURUS
April 20—May 20

- **ZODIAC CRYSTAL:** Emerald
- **SYMBOL:** The Bull
- **ELEMENT:** Earth

Whether in romantic relationships or at work, your tenacity and powerful need to take control is hidden behind a charming and seductive mask. Sensual, loving, and creative, you tune in to other people's needs and know how to please others. Unless you have three or more planets in a more adventurous sign such as Sagittarius, Aries, Gemini, or Aquarius, you prefer reliable friends and realistic goals to the mystery of the unknown, or the paradoxical whimsies in life. Hard work, practicality, management of the home, and staying down to earth can bring you abundance and financial rewards.

EMERALD
Throughout history, the emerald has been honored as a divine stone. The ancient Babylonians believed it contained a goddess, and to the Egyptians it was a symbol of eternal life and a favorite jewel of Queen Cleopatra. Derived from an ancient Persian word, translated to Greek as "Smaragdus," the emerald is a stone of love, inspiration, and infinite patience, and it embodies unity, compassion, and unconditional love. Emerald also promotes friendship and harmony, domestic bliss, contentment, and loyalty. The stone revives passion, whether for another person, a new interest, or a job. To attract romantic love, it can be worn or carried, and also enhances artistic creativity, mental focus, and clarity. It is said to be the stone of orators and philosophers.

TO REPLENISH LOVE

To call back an estranged love, speak the words you wish to say holding an emerald close to your lips, then seal the emerald in an envelope. Either keep it in a secret place or under your pillow, or, if appropriate, give it to the person when you next see them and say your message out loud.

GEMINI

May 21—June 20

○━┱ **ZODIAC CRYSTAL:** Citrine

○━┱ **SYMBOL:** Twins

○━┱ **ELEMENT:** Air

Quick-witted and versatile, you adapt to circumstances easily, are able to multitask, and love life to be easygoing, carefree, and fun. You are prone to exaggeration and are gifted with an insatiable curiosity. You act as a communicative bridge, translating ideas, talking yourself into and out of anything, and charming others with your inspired thoughts. Although not the most loyal of partners (unless you have more than three planets in a more stable sign, such as Taurus, Capricorn, Virgo), your youthful approach to life brings magic to any relationship.

CITRINE

This beautiful lemon-colored stone brings clarity, optimism, and a lively approach to life and love. It awakens creativity and imagination, and promotes the ability to manifest ideas and dreams. Often called "the Merchant's Stone," citrine is a stone of abundance, attracting wealth and prosperity, financial speculation, and commercial opportunities. If you carry a stone in your purse or handbag, it will not only attract money but also stop excess spending! Citrine brings clarity to the mind. It wakes us up to see the light and promotes zest, optimism, and meaning to your life and relationships. Light yellow crystals help new romance with vivid communication. Dark yellow citrine promotes decisiveness, precision, and persuasion.

LIGHTEN UP YOUR LIFE

Place a piece of citrine on a table or window ledge; somewhere in direct sunlight. Gaze into the crystal for a few minutes and watch the colors changing as the sun brings it to life and it begins to communicate ideas to you. As you open your mind to its powers, you will begin to feel uplifted, ready to have fun, and to go out and be noticed for your charm.

CANCER

June 21—July 22

O—• **ZODIAC CRYSTAL:** Moonstone

O—• **SYMBOL:** Crab

O—• **ELEMENT:** Water

Highly intuitive, sensitive, and aware of the natural cycles of the Universe, Cancer is the most caring and nurturing sign of the zodiac. You instinctively know how to make people feel at home, and also how to change your mood to suit their current one! Beneath the surface you're ambitious, but cautious. You care about what other people think of you, so you rarely do things on impulse and find it hard to take chances or accept change. Most important for you is to feel safe and to have a sense of belonging, whether to a family of two, or a global corporation of thousands.

MOONSTONE

Ancient legends recall how the moonstone could bring the gift of prophecy and second sight. Reflective of the moon, it could reveal the cycles of nature and mirror the rise and fall of tides even far from the sea. Known as a fertility and fidelity crystal, moonstone has been an amulet of protection for travelers, a stone of attraction for passionate lovers, and a path to intuitive wisdom.

Wearing moonstone also calms your emotions and encourages you to trust in the natural rhythms of life. It opens the mind to inspiration, serendipity, and synchronicity. It also brings positive flashes of insight, preventing you from giving up on a good idea due to negative thinking.

FOR CLARITY, INSIGHT, AND INTUITION

Lay a circle of twelve small moonstones around your bedroom and one more under your bed. These represent the lunar cycle and will also enhance your fertility or fidelity. When you go to sleep at night, take the moonstone from under your bed and place it under your pillow. When you wake in the morning, you may have a sudden flash of insight about the day ahead. Observe through the day how the "moonstone" insight is reflected in your encounters and experiences.

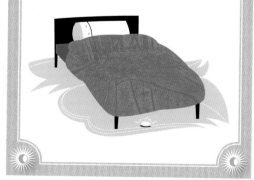

LEO
July 23—August 22

- **ZODIAC CRYSTAL:** Tiger's Eye
- **SYMBOL:** The Lion
- **ELEMENT:** Fire

Radiant, charismatic, and center-stage, Leos are proud, loyal, and determined to succeed. If you're not in the limelight, then you'll do everything in your power to put yourself there, often at the expense of others. Fiery and creative, you are talented, focused, and know instinctively when to activate a new idea or project. In love you are emotional and sexually passionate, and as you prefer glamour to the quiet life you're more likely to be a social lion than a stay-at-home cat.

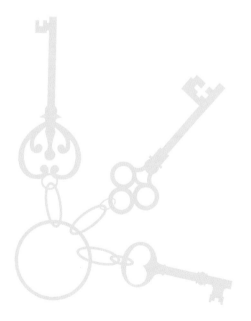

TIGER'S EYE

Like the tiger who sits and waits for its prey for a seeming eternity, tiger's eye is a stone that gives you the determination to pursue your dreams. This crystal brings you patience, tenacity, and realism. It promotes focus and a fiery realization that you can achieve your goal, knowing opportunities need to be seized when they come along. Use tiger's eye to bring clarity and remove any blockages around your creative desires.

ABUNDANCE SPELL

Tiger's eye is also used in spell work to bring money or abundance into your life. On the evening of a full moon, take a piece of tiger's eye outside and stand for two minutes with the crystal resting in the palm of your hand and hold it up to the moonlight. Repeat the following petition:

"Bless this crystal with manifesting powers, so that what I need for myself and others will come for the good of All."

Place your crystal in the southeast corner of your home for one lunar cycle to achieve good results.

VIRGO
August 23—September 22
⊶ **ZODIAC CRYSTAL:** Peridot
⊶ **SYMBOL:** The Virgin
⊶ **ELEMENT:** Earth

Discerning and discriminating, Virgo is concerned with searching for the tiny valuable gemstones of life among the waste and debris. With high standards and a critique to match, your ability to sift through the details makes you the perfect editor or forensic scientist! Yet for all your sifting, it is often in the bigger picture that the true treasure house of knowledge is to be found. You are a secret romantic, eloquent, intellectual, and self-disciplined, but your love life can often suffer when you plough all your energy into your work and career.

PERIDOT
This light olive or lime colored stone is worn by Catholic bishops as a symbol of purity and morality. Emperor Napoleon I made a gift of peridot to his wife Josephine as a symbol of his undying love and admiration. Peridot makes you more compassionate and is an excellent stone for all forms of healing, abundance, and prosperity. Wearing this stone brings a little rational common sense to romantic affairs of the heart and protects you from unnecessary

heartache or jealousy. It was once worn by ancient Egyptian priests to stop them from being envious of the Pharaoh's power. As a stone of vision, peridot clarifies your choice of destiny or purpose, and promotes clarity and well-being. It can also help to draw money and opportunities your way.

TO CLARIFY YOUR TRUE PURPOSE

Take a piece of peridot in your hand and with a magnifying glass in the other, look closely at all of its facets, colors, layers, and structure. Reflect on the intricate details of every part of this stone, then feel it in detail in your hands. Roll it around your face (if it's a polished stone) and imagine how it was once part of the earth and how every grain of sand and every stone on earth contains the universal energy. This exercise will give you a valuable experience of how discriminating peridot operates in your life.

LIBRA
September 23—October 22

o—¬ **ZODIAC CRYSTAL:** Sapphire

o—¬ **SYMBOL:** The Scales

o—¬ **ELEMENT:** Air

With your love of beauty, harmony, and peace, it's not surprising that you're diplomatic and compromising too. You negotiate with ease, and as long as you can make people happy, then you're happy too. Self-image is important to you and so is romance and love. Although you can prevaricate and often take forever to make a decision, you're great at gathering all the facts before making any promise or commitment. You find it hard to live in the here and now, preferring to idealize the future. Laid-back and seductive, you work well in a committed relationship where there is equality and a few roses round the door.

BLUE SAPPHIRE
In the ancient world, blue sapphire was the stone of spiritual hope and faith. It was a symbol of power and strength, but also of kindness and wise judgment. Known as the Wisdom Stone, ancient Greek priestesses wore it to help channel messages from the gods, while Buddhists believed it aided devotion and brought spiritual enlightenment. Wear or carry blue sapphire to promote successful lawsuits or legal affairs, whether for yourself or on behalf of someone else. Most importantly, sapphire is the stone of love, fidelity, and commitment. It brings protection, good fortune, and spiritual insight.

HOPE FOR AN ANSWER

With a piece of blue sapphire in your hand, close your eyes and relax for a few minutes. Now ask it a question that you don't know the answer to. Ask it several times over, until you feel the stone drawing in your hope for an answer. During the rest of the day observe carefully the world around you and the stone will provide you with the answer.

SCORPIO
October 23—November 21

○━▸ **ZODIAC CRYSTAL:** Obsidian

○━▸ **SYMBOL:** Scorpion

○━▸ **ELEMENT:** Water

Your mind penetrates the depths of other people's hidden motives, and your emotions run so deep that your intense passion for a subject, person, or idea becomes the focus of your life. You're powerful, erotic, mysterious, and hard to fathom. Just how you like it. Magnetic and moody, you thrive on money, sex, and power. You're not scared of the dark side of life and you're the first to rush to the rescue, but you trust no one, not even yourself. Your survival instinct is on permanent red alert and you won't be thwarted, so sometimes that sting in your tail has little choice but to hit its mark.

OBSIDIAN
All black crystals are protective, creating a "cloak of invisibility" to ward off negative energy. Obsidian also gives you a sense of your own power. It makes you feel secure, daring, and physically strong. Black obsidian with a highly polished finish can be used as a mirror for scrying—looking in the stone as a mirror to see patterns or signs to interpret the future, or to make contact with the spirit world. All forms of obsidian block geopathic stress and remove negative energy. Wearing this stone will bestow you with integrity and trust in your own goals and desires, and will keep you grounded. It enhances clarity, clears confusion, and allows you to deal with any emotional blockages with objectivity and positive thinking. A power stone, obsidian enables you to gain authority not just of yourself but in society too, so its excellent for business dealings and financial success.

EMPOWERMENT STONE

Take a piece of obsidian to work with you. Keep it in your pocket or wear it as jewelry. Every time you are confronted by a problem or a difficult contact, hold the stone and feel empowered and protected.

SAGITTARIUS

November 22—December 21

- **ZODIAC CRYSTAL:** Turquoise
- **SYMBOL:** The Archer
- **ELEMENT:** Fire

Adventurous, idealistic, restless, and passionate, Sagittarius is a sign of opportunists and those who seek meaning to life. Renowned for exaggerating or bending the truth, you make promises with utter commitment, but can't live up to the responsibility of seeing them through later on. Belief in something is essential for your well-being, whether it's a philosophy, religion, or simply your freedom. You want to explore everything and are known for your impulsive behavior and unreliable time-keeping. But you're a lover of life and you adore to be challenged by the unknown. The world is definitely your favorite oyster.

TURQUOISE

One of the oldest recorded stones in history, turquoise was the prize amulet of kings and warriors. Native American shamans wore it in ceremonies when calling upon the Great Spirit of the sky, and with its ability to change color, it was used in prophecy and divination. Turquoise is often used as a stone for protection during travel. Wear this stone to activate romantic love or to encourage spontaneity and excitement in all your romantic affairs. Turquoise enhances inner calm and creative expression, and is a great stone to carry or wear to promote your talents in the big wide world.

PROMOTE YOUR TALENTS

Place a piece of turquoise in the north area of your home; in feng shui, this direction is associated with the Career and Life Path. For three nights in a row, spend some time sitting beside your crystal and imagining the kind of career or future you want, or where you want to go in the world, and so on. On the fourth night, take the stone in your hands and believe in its power to give you a pathway to follow. Very soon you will find you have chosen a new journey.

CAPRICORN
December 22—January 19
0—➤ **ZODIAC CRYSTAL:** Garnet
0—➤ **SYMBOL:** The Goat
0—➤ **ELEMENT:** Earth

Highly principled and serious about your career or vocation, you also have a brilliant sense of humor and are often artistically or musically talented. You adore status, wealth, and the material things of life, and you have a powerful need to get to the top of your particular profession. Although you conform to conventional expectations, as you get older and wiser, you become not only more youthful in your outlook but more radical, too. Emotionally you don't give much away, but once you allow someone to get close, you make the perfect power behind the throne—or on it.

GARNET
The Greeks called garnet the Lamp Stone, because if worn as a necklace, it was believed that the wearer had the power to see in the dark. A crystal of sensuality and passion, garnet heals emotional rifts between lovers and evokes strong, intense feelings. Wearing garnet balances your energy, bringing serenity or passion, whichever is required. Garnet is considered a lucky stone for love, success, and for business

relationships. It boosts self-confidence, stimulates desires, and uplifts your moods to positive ones. Carry or wear garnet to dissolve fears of insecurity and avoid money loss. Lucky for love, success, and for achieving your goals, this crystal can be used to increase your popularity and enhance your self-esteem. It also promotes success in the world of business and creates beneficial associates.

SEEING THE WAY FORWARD

In the evening, once it is dark, turn out all the lights and calm your mind as you get used to the blackness. Then hold up this stone in front of your eyes. As your eyes get accustomed to the blackness, the stone will slowly appear to "glow" dark red. According to ancient Greek and Roman mythology, it can be used as a lamp or torch to guide you. Maybe try it out and see if it gives you the power to illuminate the way?

AQUARIUS

January 20—February 18

○━ **ZODIAC CRYSTAL:** Amber

○━ **SYMBOL:** The Water Bearer

○━ **ELEMENT:** Air

Futuristic and concerned with humanity, Aquarius is a sign of altruism and freedom for all. Unconventional and often radical in your views, you can also be dogmatic and judgmental. You have original and often quirky ideas, but can be scattered and disorganized, preferring organized chaos to responsibility and duty. Although you love talking about feelings, you don't like feeling them! Unconditional love is hugely important to you and if you do ever commit yourself to an exclusive relationship, you insist on having friends of both sexes. Friendship and amity are as precious as gold in your life. So is work, whether you're feeding the world, or saving the whales.

AMBER

Amber is technically not a gemstone or mineral, but a fossilized sap from prehistoric trees that has solidified over the course of millions of years. Asian cultures regard amber as the "soul of the tiger," in that it helps to manifest desires, heightens intellectual abilities, and gives clarity of thought and wisdom. It is reputed to cleanse its environment by drawing out negativity and to relieve physical pain in the same way. It brings the energies of patience, protection, psychic shielding, romantic love, sensuality, purification, balance, healing, and calmness to those who wear or carry it. It is also considered a good luck charm for love and marriage.

CLEANSING THE SPIRIT

Wear amber for a week and notice how you begin to feel better about yourself. Not only that, but you are less negative, you react more objectively to situations, and you can see the world from a wider perspective.

PISCES
February 19—March 20
- **ZODIAC CRYSTAL:** Amethyst
- **SYMBOL:** The Fish
- **ELEMENT:** Water

Whether a dreaming visionary or a talented artist, Pisces can climb the dizzy heights of success, often giving it all up when led astray or charmed by romance. Idealistic and imaginative, you're a sensitive soul who needs to live and work in a laid-back environment. Romantic and seductive, you fall in love with love, or fall into the victim–savior trap, playing either one or the other role in an attempt to define your own emotional boundaries and find your true identity. Kind, gullible, but elusive and unreliable, you give all of your time to helping the underdog.

AMETHYST

Ancient Greeks and Romans routinely studded their goblets with this beautiful purple crystal, believing that wine drunk from the cup was powerless to intoxicate them. This crystal of romance, creativity, and spirituality also promises a realistic attitude. Reputed to control evil thoughts and increase intelligence, it enhances your creativity and passion.

Wearing or carrying the crystal helps to stir your imagination and intuitive powers, refining thought and helping to stimulate new ideas. Amethyst is an excellent stone for diplomats, negotiators, and business people. Wear or carry the crystal to promote spiritual insight, intellectual reasoning, and all the magic of the Universe that can help make dreams come true.

GET CLOSER TO THE UNIVERSE

Take a glass cup or wine goblet and fill with pure spring water. Place a piece of amethyst at the bottom of the glass. Gaze into the water and see the amethyst and its powerful color radiate through the reflections of the glass and water. Now close your eyes and imagine the color permeating every part of your body, spirit, and soul, and so feeling at one with the Universe.

WORKING WITH CRYSTALS

You've now got to know twenty-two of the most popular and useful crystals. Now you're going to see which of these, plus some newcomers to the list, can be worked into various themes in daily life. You'll discover how to make crystals a very important part of your life as you place them in the home, use them for spell or ritual work, or carry them for specific purposes.

STRENGTHENING THE AURA

Before working with crystals, it's important to strengthen your aura and subtle body energy (also known as the life force, "chi," or simply the "spiritual you") as these are the invisible forces or energy that connect you to both the crystal's power and the Universe. Practice this simple exercise before any work with crystals to empower and align yourself with their energies.

1. Hold a piece of white quartz crystal in each hand, sit comfortably, and breathe deeply and slowly. Focus on your hands and open up to the power of the crystal energy. Feel this permeate your whole body and then radiate through your physical body and into your auric field.

2. Concentrate on this merging and replenishing of spiritual energy for several minutes.

3. Make a daily affirmation:

"I love my spiritual being, because I love myself."

CRYSTAL PLACEMENT

In the ancient art of feng shui, crystals are placed in various positions in the house according to a grid system with regard to the flow of universal energy around the home and in the environment. This was determined by the compass directions, which make up the octagonal and magical bagua.

These directions are considered auspicious for various aspects of your life, and by placing the crystal associated with a direction in the corresponding area of the home, you will benefit from the crystal's energizing and harmonious powers. For example, if you place a garnet in the southwest corner of your home, you will dramatically improve your love relationships.

The following pages include rituals for various aspects of your life, such as to enhance relationships, home life, career, personal power, or success. In this way, you can practice using crystals straight away for your benefit.

Most of the crystals are readily available. Imagine working with crystals as if you were working with your favorite colleagues or friends, and you will soon start to understand you are part of the tapestry of the Universe too.

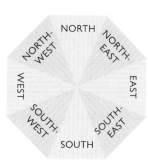

BAGUA DIRECTIONS	KEYWORDS	CRYSTALS TO BOOST THESE AREAS
South ↓	○—⚡ Fame ○—⚡ Success ○—⚡ Reputation	RUBY
Southwest ↙	○—⚡ Marriage ○—⚡ Romance ○—⚡ Happiness	ROSE QUARTZ
West ←	○—⚡ Children ○—⚡ Creativity	AZURITE
Northwest ↖	○—⚡ Communication ○—⚡ Friends ○—⚡ Mentors	CALCITE
North ↑	○—⚡ Career ○—⚡ Professional	AVENTURINE
Northeast ↗	○—⚡ Education ○—⚡ Knowledge	TURQUOISE
East →	○—⚡ Family ○—⚡ Wellbeing	ONYX
Southeast ↘	○—⚡ Wealth ○—⚡ Prosperity	MALACHITE

NEW ROMANCE/LOVE/SEX

Garnets inspire romance, sapphires commitment and fidelity, and watermelon tourmaline, emotional and spiritual love. Wear or carry one each of garnet, sapphire, and watermelon tourmaline every day. Place a garnet under your pillow to ignite intimacy and a sapphire in your living room to revitalize emotional warmth and compassion.

KEY SECRET

To meet the lover of your dreams, carry seven (in numerology the number seven is associated with unexpected intriguing encounters) garnets wrapped in a piece of paper with the words "I love you forever" written on the inside of the paper.

FOR ROMANCE

For romantic success, sit comfortably and place a piece of rose quartz on a surface in front of you for a few moments as you relax. Now take it in your hands and gaze at the crystal for several minutes as you repeat either in your head or out loud, "I am of Fire, and of Fire I will burn brightly. May this clarity flow through all hearts as well as my own." Keep your rose quartz on a south-facing window ledge to attract love to you.

ATTRACTION

WHAT YOU WILL NEED:

- A bowl
- Rose petals
- Two pieces of red carnelian or garnet
- Red candle
- Bloodstone
- Mirror

1. To enhance your outer charisma and attract love to you, you need to incorporate some fire energy into your world. Fill a small bowl with red rose petals and place a piece of red carnelian or garnet on top of the petals. Light a red candle and as you run your fingers through the petals, affirm to yourself:

"I need to learn to express my love to receive that of others. With this stone I will be loved for who I am."

2. Next, place another piece of carnelian or garnet on a low table or shelf. Place a mirror behind the crystal to magnify its qualities in your direction. Every day for a week, sit quietly in front of the mirror for a few minutes, holding the crystal in your hands to fill you with passion and desire and to prepare you for the romantic encounters you're about to have.

A DYNAMIC SEX LIFE

To encourage a dynamic sex life, wear or carry fire agate or ruby during the day, and then place it in your bedroom in the south area of your room, or under your pillow, to awaken your own sexuality and attract others to you.

DEEPER COMMITMENT

WHAT YOU WILL NEED:

- Six pieces of green tourmaline
- Six small pieces of clear quartz crystal
- Two white candles

1. To improve or cement your relationship, place six pieces of green tourmaline in the symbolic pattern shown below, interspersed by six small pieces of clear quartz crystal, which amplify the energy through their vibrational force.

2. Place two white candles on either side of the crystal oracle and light them every night for four nights. Each time, meditate and concentrate on your lover and you, as you stare at the crystals. To promote a truly committed relationship, imagine you are dancing arm in arm among the crystals.

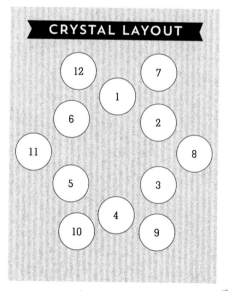

CRYSTAL LAYOUT

- green tourmaline 1–6
- clear quartz 7–12

RELATIONSHIP PROBLEMS

Carry or wear tiger's eye to enhance your personal energy, and amber or green aventurine to dissociate yourself from negative people, bonds, or situations. Place a piece of obsidian under your bed to strengthen your self-belief and ability to move on.

KEY SECRET:

On a full moon night, place a piece of green aventurine on a photo of someone who is trying to manipulate you in order to block or banish their psychic energy. Leave it there for one lunar cycle.

RELATIONSHIP GOING NOWHERE

WHAT YOU WILL NEED:

- Imperial topaz or obsidian
- Piece of green aventurine
- Five pieces of amazonite

1. To help end a relationship that's going nowhere, place a piece of imperial topaz or obsidian in the east or south corner of your living area to promote and manifest your goal. Wear or carry a piece of green aventurine during the day to protect you against unwanted contact from the one you are intending to leave.

2. Next, place five pieces of amazonite in a circle on your table or a place where they won't be disturbed. Every day for four days, turn each stone in a clockwise direction at a ninety-degree angle, until on the fourth day they are back in their original position. This will encourage positive energy to help you break up or shake off bad relationships and gain good ones.

3. Each time you turn the stones, repeat the following: "For the good of myself and all the best for the future for you, I turn these stones full circle, to weave our lives apart. So mote it be."

TO DETRACT AN ADMIRER

In the east corner of your home, place five pieces of peridot in the shape of the points of a pentagram (see diagram below). This will promote emotional distance and strengthen your own personal aura of protection. After one week return to the site and turn each stone three hundred and sixty degrees clockwise. After the second week, turn the stones back three hundred and sixty degrees counterclockwise. As you do so, repeat the following: "Peridot spirit, for those to whom I can't be true, let it be so that they go too." As you end the ritual you will detract the unwanted admirer for good.

CRYSTAL LAYOUT

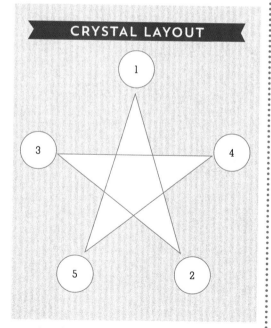

• peridot placed in this order

DEALING WITH JEALOUSY

You can use this spell to banish your own jealous heart, or another's—as long as neither of you is actually cheating on the other. This spell only works if the jealousy is rooted in fear of rejection, low self-esteem, or other psychological issues.

WHAT YOU WILL NEED:
• A piece of chrysoprase
• Two green candles

1. Light the two candles, then take the crystal between your hands. As you watch the candles flicker for a few minutes, repeat this spell:

> *"No longer jealous shall I be*
> *No longer jealous shall you be.*
> *No longer jealousy shall move us*
> *No longer jealousy shall prove us.*
> *Begone, jealous heart,*
> *with chrysoprase;*
> *The deed is done, let's mend our ways."*

2. Kiss the stone and wear or carry it for one lunar cycle to lift you from jealous imaginings.

FOR CREATIVITY AND SUCCESS

To promote creative ideas, place either a diamond (if you can afford a real one) or a piece of clear topaz in your work desk drawer, or in the area of your home where you do most of your work. This will also boost clarity and focus.

KEY SECRET:

Carry or wear azurite on a daily basis to empower you with deep insights.

FOR IMAGINATIVE THINKING

To bring beautiful, imaginative thoughts into your mind, wear or carry a combination of turquoise, aquamarine, and calcite. Take these three crystals and place them on a table in front of you. First, hold the piece of turquoise in your left hand, close your eyes, and let thoughts flow in and through your mind without attaching yourself to them. Imagine the color turquoise. After a minute, open your eyes and replace the turquoise. Now take up the aquamarine. Do the same thing, feeling the vibrational energy permeating your hand as you meditate upon the color aquamarine. Finally, do the same with the piece of calcite. These crystal energies will enhance your imaginative powers and creative skill.

Remember these three crystals as follows:

- Turquoise opens you up to the universal storehouse of knowledge, directly linked to the imagination.
- Aquamarine gives you courage to explore those illuminating thoughts.
- Calcite allows you to discriminate and bring those ideas to life.

You may soon find that you are inspired by anything, from seeing an old lady smile, to hearing a bird singing.

FOR SUCCESSFUL NEGOTIATIONS

When dealing with others we need to exude both compassion and our own inner self-worth. First, vitalize your charisma. Place a piece of green tourmaline in your bedroom, in your car, and on your work desk. Be totally honest about believing in both yourself and the power of universal attraction, and you will be able to negotiate successfully. To make sure that your negotiating power is followed through, leading you to a brighter future, take seven pieces of white quartz crystal and place them on a table or window ledge in the shape of the symbol shown below (associated with charismatic rewards). The main points should all be facing south, as well as the top end of the symbol. Trace your finger around this pattern in a clockwise direction every day for seven days and repeat the mantra, "Harmony and negotiation will bring me peace and reward."

CRYSTAL LAYOUT

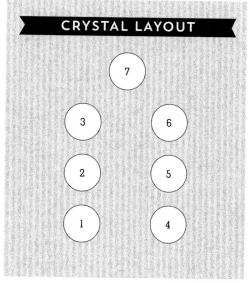

• white quartz placed in this order

PERSONAL ASPIRATION

This ritual will promote self-focus and success and strengthen your own sense of identity too.

WHAT YOU WILL NEED:

• A gold or gold-colored metal ring
• A piece of tiger's eye
• A white cloth
• A piece of paper and pen

1. Place the gold ring and piece of tiger's eye on a piece of white cloth, preferably outside to capture the pure light of the Universe. The white cloth can be draped over a wall, fence, large boulder, or garden seat, but it must be raised above ground as a symbol of celestial travel rather than earthbound travel.

2. Stand or sit before your crystal and when your mind is calm, repeat three times:

> *"I flow with the cosmos, and wherever it will take me now, will lead me to my dream aspiration and success."*

3. Write this affirmation on the piece of paper and keep it in a drawer or near where you work, along with your gold ring or tiger's eye, and wait for the magic to begin.

GETTING RESULTS

Hematite will enable you to ground your plans, blue topaz to manifest them, and blue lace agate to communicate them. Wear and carry all three, and place six of each in a small pouch in your desk or workplace to ensure success.

KEY SECRET:

To maximize your ability to manifest results, place a piece of jasper near your main entrance door so it empowers you every time you enter or leave.

REALIZING GOALS

Take five pieces of azurite for clarity of purpose and place them on the ground covering an area of about two feet, in the layout shown below, with the main points of the crystals facing east. Every day, stand at the easternmost end of the symbol and look in an easterly direction and affirm, "My goals are favorable, my gain is for me, but I give thanks for all that I receive and will return it with love."

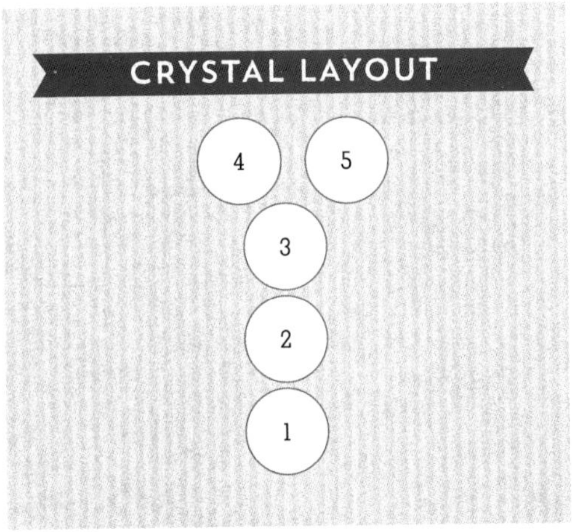

CRYSTAL LAYOUT

```
    4    5

       3

       2

       1
```

• white quartz placed in this order

ATTRACTING MENTORS

To align yourself with beneficial outside influences and to ensure good communication with others, wear or carry a piece of lapis lazuli. If you feel you need to be more objective about who is useful to you, and who may not have your best interests at heart, place a piece of jade on your desk. Every time you sit down to work, pick up the jade and hold it for a few seconds to imbue you with its discerning qualities.

REVIVING PASSION FOR WORK

To revive passion for work, zest for living, or enthusiasm for a new interest, keep a piece of fire opal in your desk. It will encourage dynamic professional interaction. Fire opal also bestows initiative and new ideas. It awakens your own inner fire, so that you can accomplish much more in a short time and simultaneously fire others with enthusiasm.

MANIFESTING ACHIEVEMENT

For this to work, you really, really must believe it!

WHAT YOU WILL NEED:

• Three pieces of imperial topaz
• A green candle
• A purple candle

1. Place three pieces of imperial topaz on a table in the shape of an equilateral triangle with the point of the triangle to the top. Place one green candle on the left and a purple candle on the right of the triangle.

2. Every evening for five nights, light the candles for three minutes, while you concentrate on the symbol before you. The green candle will invoke the power of manifestation and the purple candle, ambition and achievement.

3. After you have meditated on the symbol for three minutes, repeat the following:

"Thank you both crystals and the power of Fire which connect me to the Universe. All I ask is that I can manifest both achievement and success."

PROMOTING TALENT

To promote your talents, place a piece of moonstone on your kitchen or bedroom window ledge. Wear amber during the day to cleanse yourself of negativity and improve your self-confidence. To enhance these placements, you can perform a simple ritual. Draw a hexagram (see diagram below) onto a piece of paper. Take six small pieces of amethyst and wrap them in the paper. Place the bundle in the north corner of your home to encourage all career and talent opportunities.

HEXAGRAM

SELF-EMPOWERMENT

One of the most empowering crystals is the luscious black onyx, which promotes personal strength. It bestows order and self-awareness and converts subjective value to objective acceptance. Onyx enhances the ability to be in control of your own destiny, no longer beholden to other people's expectations.

KEY SECRET:

Wear or carry onyx every day to help you to concentrate and see clearly the truth of every situation.

GOOD LUCK SELF-EMPOWERMENT

Although stones such as onyx and obsidian are great for enhancing your inner power, there are other stones that will amplify and expand the range of power you need for specific opportunities or events. For example, luck will be on your side if you add citrine for abundance, sodalite to help you make intuitive decisions on financial opportunities, and rhodochrosite to amplify self-confidence in your choices. Place six pieces of citrine on your desk or in a drawer near where you work. Each time you sit down to work or communicate your plans to anyone, touch the stones one by one and thank the stones and the Universe for the good luck that is to come.

UNLEASH YOUR POWER

To free yourself from the power others might have over you, wear or carry protective amethyst and shungite. To boost confidence and free yourself from any emotional vulnerability, carry or wear bloodstone to give you courage and strength.

Place three pieces of chalcedony in a tiny box and place it under your bed; this will calm your emotions and help you to sleep better, preparing you for a new day of self-belief and confidence in what you can achieve.

TRUSTING OTHERS

For successful negotiations with people you don't know, or don't trust, wear or carry sodalite for intuitive understanding, and jasper to help you to stand up for your beliefs or opinions. Carry or wear green jade to help you to discern exactly what's going on and to get your priorities in order.

EMPOWERING YOUR SPIRITUAL SELF

Apart from our "mind" self, we have a spiritual self too. And we need to nourish and nurture it, for it is the part of us that connects us to the deeper mysteries of the Universe.

WHAT YOU WILL NEED:

• Five pieces of selenite
• Two white candles

1. Place the five pieces of selenite on a table in the pattern of the pentagram (see page 71), a magical symbol of the cosmos.

2. Light the two candles, and place one to the east of the pentagram and one to the west.

3. Relax and concentrate on the candle flames for a minute or so to still your mind. Then take each crystal in turn in your hands, and as you do so repeat the following:

"My spiritual self will stay with me even when I am being ruthless.
Love is all around me; I know it is there to benefit me.
I believe in the life force that heals all.
The power of belief is mine to give to others and to myself.
With these crystals I will empower and keep safe my soul."

4. When you have held all five crystals in your hands, place them in a safe place. Every time you feel you want to be more in touch with your spiritual self or need to draw on your intuition, take each crystal in your hands again for a few seconds and you will be re-empowered.

FAME AND FORTUNE

Many of us secretly want fame of some kind, and most of us would like enough fortune to keep us content and secure. To maximize your reputation, sense of fame, and as much fortune as the Universe can give you, place five uncut rubies or pieces of red sardonyx in the south area of your home.

KEY SECRET:

If you crave fame in a creative or public performance-related area, wear or carry lapis lazuli to allow you to take on any role in the world.

BE A STAR

Place a gilt- or silver-framed mirror against an interior wall of your home so that the mirror is facing south. Then place a diamond, piece of selenite, or white quartz crystal in front of the mirror. These crystals will improve your image and bring you the success you deserve. Wear or carry pink tourmaline or rose quartz to encourage groups of other people to adore you and to boost your reputation. If you're looking to be center stage, or literally on the stage, you will also need to carry or wear a few pieces of rhodochrosite and fire agate to enhance your charisma.

BE IN THE LIMELIGHT

WHAT YOU WILL NEED:
- Eight bloodstones
- A length of twine or string

1. Place the bloodstones on a window ledge or table, in the same pattern as the symbol below. Bloodstones promote the strength you need to stand out from the crowd and this medieval magic symbol encourages fame and fortune.

CRYSTAL LAYOUT

1	5
2	6
3	7
4	8

2. Circle the two parallel lines of the symbol with a piece of twine to protect the energy. After two weeks, remove the stones and leave one bloodstone in the middle of the twine circle for another lunar cycle. This symbolizes your "stage" and will give you the energy to work successfully with large groups of people and promote fortunate encounters.

TO FEEL BLESSED

WHAT YOU WILL NEED:

- One piece of moonstone
- One piece of rose quartz
- Pen and paper
- A small box

1. To really feel blessed with beauty, vitality and love, write the following statements on a piece of paper, filling in the blanks according to your own desires.

I am really pleased when I...
I adore...
I'm fascinated by...
I enjoy...
I am grateful for...
I want...
Warm feelings come to me when...
I feel joy when...
I intend to...
My purpose is...

2. Next, place the moonstone in the south and the rose quartz in the southwest areas of your home to enhance all aspects of your self-image.

3. During the crescent moon, when the outer edge of the moon is lit up on its right side, place the stones on a window ledge to align with intuitive, nurturing lunar energy. Remove and place them under your pillow until the full moon and you will be blessed with love from others. Once the full moon has passed, put the stones back in the south and southwest areas of your home. Every time you feel you need to "recharge" your vitality or need to feel loved, do the same moon cycle ritual.

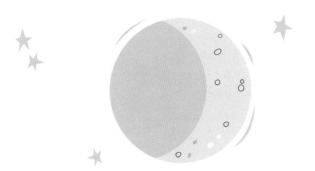

FAMILY/HOME

One of the most important places in our lives is our home, or our sense of what "home" means to us. Placing crystals in the home has been part of the ritual work you've been doing so far; to make the home itself harmonious, here are some important rituals to perform.

KEY SECRET:

In the east corner or area of your home, place black tourmaline to protect you from difficult energy in general and to keep all negativity at bay.

PROTECTION AGAINST GEOPATHIC STRESS

Geopathic stress refers to the interference of disturbing or negative energy within the environment, usually in the ground. This can be caused by underground water courses and springs, electric cables, underground train lines, fissures in the bedrock, and even living near Native American burial grounds or cemeteries. To protect your home from this kind of negativity, a "grid" of crystals can be laid, surrounding the home to form a web of positive energy to counterbalance any unwanted energy. This is known as earth acupuncture. It follows the same principles as Chinese acupuncture, where the earth's meridians are aligned with crystals to create balance in your environment.

As very few of us are likely to be able to lay a ring of crystals right round our homes, I have provided this simple indoor ritual. The circle of stones is symbolic of the larger grid and will have a similar influence.

In the southeast area of your home, place seven pieces of white quartz crystal in a circle. In the center place a piece of moonstone. Then repeat the following mantra for five minutes with your eyes closed:

> *"This home will be safe from all that wish to intrude, and all negativity be gone."*

Then open your eyes and thank the crystals.

HARMONIOUS FAMILY LIFE

To make your home stress-free and harmonious, create a sacred place in the north corner of a room. Cover a small table with silk or voile in a shade of Prussian blue, dark blue, or aquamarine. Hang up above it, or lean against the wall, a painting of waves at sea or a waterfall—as long as the water is "moving." Place two pieces of blue agate or lapis lazuli on the table to promote beneficial energy in all you do and encourage good relationships among family members.

TO REVITALIZE THE HOME

WHAT YOU WILL NEED:
- One piece of smoky quartz
- Two pieces of amethyst
- One piece of onyx

1. First, walk around all the rooms in your home and clap your hands briskly. This shifts energy and "airs" the home of all dull, stale, or negative emotions and difficult energies. Don't forget to clap in dark corners, under stairs, in cupboards, and as high as you can above your head. Clap a rhythm, like a drum beat, and the vibrant energy will shift negativity and create a refreshed home.

2. Next, place a piece of smoky quartz in the west area of your home to bring happiness to children and all creative endeavors.

3. Place a piece of amethyst in the west and east, for general protection from unwanted electromagnetic fields. Wear or carry amethyst during the day. If you are going through any difficult family situations, you can also place shungite, which protects against any bleak perspective, in the east corner of your home.

4. Finally, place a piece of onyx on the window ledge of your kitchen or bedroom to promote well-being and protection to all.

CHAPTER THREE

THE KEY to CRYSTALS AND DIVINATION

- Crystals help you to create your own destiny
- Cast crystals onto a zodiac circle to reveal your future
- Discover how intuitive you are
- Learn which crystals will protect you from negativity

HOW TO USE CRYSTALS FOR DIVINATION

L ike other divination tools such as the tarot, runes, palmistry, and numerology, crystals are simply a "bridge" between the part of your mind that has intuitive and psychic ability (attributed to the left side of the brain) and the universal storehouse of knowledge (also known as the collective unconscious), which knows all things past, present, and future.

Divination, rooted in the Latin word "*divinare*," meaning "to foresee, to be inspired by a god," is also related to "*divinus*," or divine. Divination is the method of gaining insight into a question or situation using secret or occult practices and rituals. It's not so much about looking to the future as simply revealing a truth, whether about the current moment, a future one, or a past one. After all, our linear perception of time is severely subjective, as any quantum physicist or mystic knows.

Crystals help you to get in touch with the untapped source of power that is hidden deep within you. This is your direct link to the universal energy drawn from all the cosmos at any given moment. With their subtle vibrational living energy, they open the gateway to your resonance to the cosmos and allow you to access your own inner wisdom and develop your mystic powers.

You may already have some sense of this intuitive side of your nature; for example, when you get a gut reaction that something is about to happen, or "know" who is about to call you on the phone. This kind of divine foresight is innate to all of us. The process of divination gets you in touch with this unconscious pathway. So, treat divination with an open mind and an open heart, and enjoy discovering how to "see" the answer or to just "know" what is the right decision to take in any difficult situation.

HOW INTUITIVE ARE YOU?

Take this quiz to discover how intuitive you are. Look at the questions and for each one pick one of the following answers:

Yes, often = 3 points
Sometimes = 2 points
No, never = 1 point

Do you reach for the phone just as someone else is about to call you?

Can you "see round corners," or, in other words, know who or what you're going to meet as you turn down a street?

Are your first instinctive impressions of people usually right?

Do you believe in magic?

Is mind over matter more important to you than physical strength?

Do you analyze your dreams?

Have any of your dreams come true?

Do you believe that universal or cosmic energy flows through everything?

Do you ever use tarot, or other divination tools?

If yes, are you surprised by the accuracy of the readings?

Do you feel instantly "in tune" with certain people, as if you've known each other in some other realm?

Now add up the points and check your intuition rating:

Over 20: You already have a great level of psychic ability.
13–19: Your intuition is about average, so it's time to work on developing your powers.
12 or under: You may be uncertain or skeptical, so do some work with crystals that can enhance your spiritual nature (see pages 160–169).

ORACLES AND PSYCHIC POWER

Crystals are like oracles; they speak a language from the Universe through their color, their vibrations and resonance, and their correspondence to our own flashes of insight when we reconnect to the Universe. They simply reaffirm what we already know deep within ourselves.

Crystals can be cast onto a zodiac circle to harness the power of the planetary forces, or they can be laid out in spreads in a similar way to the tarot and runes.

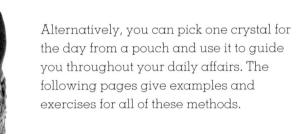

Alternatively, you can pick one crystal for the day from a pouch and use it to guide you throughout your daily affairs. The following pages give examples and exercises for all of these methods.

DEVELOP YOUR INTUITIVE POWER

To help you to develop your intuitive powers, try this simple exercise to connect to the natural energy of the crystals and to get to know the ones which "mean something" to you.

1. Take seven crystals of any color or type but all of about the same shape and size. Sit down at a table. Relax and calm your mind.

2. Close your eyes and move the crystals around randomly so that you don't know which ones are which. With your eyes still closed, place the crystals in a horizontal line on the table in front of you, without thinking too much about the order and making sure you have all seven before you.

3. Now run your fingers backward and forward along the line of crystals until you feel one of the crystals "calling" to you. Perhaps one feels warmer than others, or you just know the right crystal as your finger moves up and down the line.

4. Before you open your eyes, take the crystal in your hand and concentrate on what it makes you feel. Sad, happy, angry, excited, furious, curious? This should be an instant intuitive flash of a feeling. If you have to start thinking or analyzing your reaction, then put the crystal back on the table and start again.

5. Once you have had your "flash" of insight, open your eyes and look at the crystal. Is it telling you anything different now that you can see it with your eyes? Does its color, shape, or quality match your intuitive response to it?

6. Do this with various crystals every day or evening for a week, until you eventually "see" that what your intuition is telling you aligns with the crystal's specific powers.

PSYCHIC PROTECTION

When you start to work with divination and crystals, you are obviously opening yourself up to other psychic energy—not just from the people around you, but also from the spiritual contact you make with the Universe.

Sometimes we walk into a room and intuitively know that someone is not all they seem, or we pick up hostility in the atmosphere, or simply the spiritual residue of difficult or traumatic emotions from those who once lived in a house. It is important to employ psychic protection techniques before entering into any divination with crystals or any other tools. Any of the following simple techniques can be used if you feel vulnerable due to negative people around you or their bad vibrations.

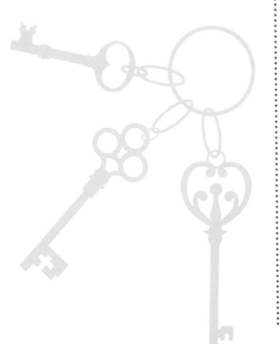

PROTECTION RITUAL

Wear a piece of amethyst, fluorite, or black obsidian, or hold a piece in your hands. As you become calm and focused, imagine that a golden light begins to emanate from the crystal's very core. Slowly it gets bigger and bigger, until it creates a huge bubble of light around you. As it gradually expands to completely contain you and the crystal, you feel safe, protected, and sure that wherever you go with this crystal, whether by carrying it or wearing it, you only have to touch and hold it to reignite the bubble of protection around you.

If you ever feel you have entered a difficult environment, hold your crystal for a few seconds to restore the golden bubble's power and be protected from any negative or hostile influence. Before starting your crystal readings or any other divinatory work, place the crystal on the table and thank it for its blessing and protection. Then, take it in your hands and hold it for two minutes to empower you with its protective energy.

PROTECTION CRYSTALS

Here are some other crystals which are used for specific forms of protection.

PROTECTION FROM THE EVIL EYE	PROTECTION FROM NEGATIVE ENERGY	PROTECTION FOR CHILDREN	PROTECTION DURING TRAVEL
TIGER'S EYE	BLACK ONYX	BLUE LACE AGATE	AQUAMARINE *(at sea)*
CARNELIAN	CITRINE	JADE	MALACHITE *(flying)*
MALACHITE	JET	RUBY	GARNET *(on land)*

PERSONAL ENERGY PROTECTION	PROTECTION FROM DARK SPIRITS AND SPELLS	PROTECTION FOR THE HOME
LABRADORITE	BLACK SAPPHIRE	WHITE QUARTZ *(general)*
SUNSTONE	CHRYSOBERYL	RUBY *(family and possessions)*
FIRE AGATE	HEMATITE	SARDONYX *(against crime)*

A CRYSTAL FOR THE DAY

M ost divination revolves around a question that you or a friend asks, and the crystal as an oracle "tells" you the answer. It may be a question related to the past, the future, or the present.

Whatever the question, make it straightforward and not loaded with emotion. For example, say you're in a job, and feel frustrated, restless, let down, or just bored—but can't see any way out of it at the moment. A bad question would be: "Is it better if I resign or put up with the bad vibes?" (You can see the querent has already put a value judgment on the job with its "bad vibes.") A good question would be, "If I resign this job, will I be happy?" Or, "If I stay in this job, will I be happy?"

When using crystals for day-ahead divination, obviously the only question you really need to ask is, "What kind of day am I going to have?" You can make it far more positive by including something that "you want" to happen during the day, something attainable: for example, a productive day, a round of applause from colleagues, an easy ride to work on the tram, and so on. As long as it is possible, then with the help of your trusted crystal you can make your own magic happen, and divine your own future day.

It's a new day. What do you want to happen?

DAY-AHEAD DIVINATION

Hopefully, by now you will have a pouch or box in which you can keep a selection of the twenty-two crystals we've so far looked at in detail. As long as you have at least ten, you'll be able to use them for day-ahead divination.

1. Place the crystals in the pouch and gently shake or move them around with your fingers without looking at them.

2. Close your eyes, relax, and think about what you wish. Start simple. For example: "I wish to meet a beautiful stranger who smiles at me and makes my day!"

3. Keep repeating your wish over and over again in your mind, as you put your hand into the pouch and touch all the stones until you find one that "speaks" to you. Keep saying your wish as you draw the stone from the bag.

4. Open your eyes and look at the stone in your hand. Now comes the fascinating bit. Obviously you have to "read" an answer from the stone. But it isn't just going to show you an image or symbol like a tarot card. In fact, it's the crystal's color symbolism and unique qualities that encapsulate the oracle. On the next pages you will see interpretations for all the twenty-two crystals we have concentrated on in this book so far, and you'll see how they can be interpreted as a forecast of the kind of energy you can expect for the day ahead. So say I've chosen amber. How do I interpret this in relation to my question? Amber is about ideas, radical thoughts, and unusual encounters. Amber is asking to be taken along with you during the day to activate that radical encounter, which suggests your wish may come true.

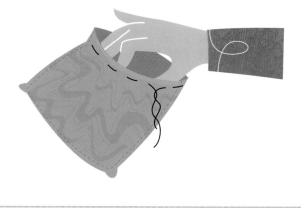

DAY-AHEAD ORACLES

Here are some brief interpretations for the kind of energy you can expect when you choose a crystal for the day.

ORANGE CARNELIAN

Indicates progressive thinking. You will break free from conventional ideas or habits.

ONYX

Material gain and new values. Financial reward can also be expected.

TOPAZ

Assists decision-making, good for traveling, and great for communicating ideas.

TOURMALINE

Attracts people and new romance to you.

LAPIS LAZULI

The "eye of wisdom." Indicates career success and new insight.

OPAL

Gets you more in touch with what others are feeling or thinking. Makes you more aware of your own desires.

BLUE LACE AGATE

Gives great clarity and life-changing contacts.

RED AGATE

Gives you a shot of courage and powerful initiative. Helps you prove a point.

CLEAR QUARTZ

The action crystal. You'll get things done and start new projects.

AMETHYST

A passionate encounter will be beneficial or transform your life.

MOONSTONE

Trust in your intuition; emotional strength will win through.

MALACHITE

Resolution of money issues; success in joint affairs.

RED CARNELIAN

Brings adventure, inventive friends, and beneficial challenges.

TIGER'S EYE

Dare to be different or dramatic in love; indicates a fiery admirer.

TURQUOISE

Travel imminent; love is boundless.

ROSE QUARTZ

Helps you to improve relationships or to meet the perfect partner.

PERIDOT

You can make a serious choice; work opportunities beckon.

OBSIDIAN

Changes for the better; professional success or job promotion.

CITRINE

Travel is favored, quick decisions can be made successfully.

JADE

A seductive stranger takes you by surprise; indecisive about love.

AMBER

Radical ideas will work; be open-minded to new ideas.

SIMPLE CRYSTAL READING METHOD

One method for consulting the crystals is to simply place all your crystals in a pouch or bag. If you can, try to include a piece of clear quartz crystal to represent clarity, and a piece of amethyst for beneficial change. If you choose these, then they are doubly important for you.

DRAWING THE CRYSTALS

Sit quietly and close your eyes. Focus on a question or issue, for example, "Will new romance come my way?" Put your hand inside the pouch and take your first piece of crystal. As you feel inside, handle the crystals gently until you feel as if one is speaking to you. Place each crystal on the table or floor in front of you in a horizontal line.

- The first is the crystal of illumination, representing your current self and the energy you are radiating to the world.
- Take another crystal. This is the crystal of darkness, representing outside influences, people, or blockages.
- The third crystal is the crystal of fortune, which represents the outcome of your question.

EXAMPLE READING

When you have drawn all three crystals, use the keywords and phrases given on the following pages to do your reading. Here is an example interpretation to help you.

Question: Is love coming my way?
1. Crystal of illumination: Citrine
   Your current communication talents will help you to find romance.
2. Crystal of darkness: Red Carnelian
   Watch out for pushy friends who may think they know what's best for you.
3. Crystal of fortune: Amber
   An unusual or unexpected encounter will prove to bring you the kind of person you're looking for.

CRYSTAL LAYOUT

(1) (2) (3)

1   2   3

MORE EXAMPLE READINGS

The following readings will give you an idea of the different types of questions you can ask. Rather than ask the crystals to make a choice for you, learn to ask questions that have a simple response and help you to make your own decisions or to reach a conclusion. For example, instead of asking, "Shall I move abroad, or should I stay here?", say "Is this a favorable time to move abroad?"

Question: Is it the right time to look for a career change?

We often seek change, but are fearful of it. Yet opening up to the truth that you do want to make a dramatic lifestyle change is often the very catalyst which allows you to do so.

1. **Crystal of illumination: Peridot**
   You know if you make an effort there are work opportunities out there.
2. **Crystal of darkness: Rose quartz**
   Don't be swayed by people who say they know what's best for you.
3. **Crystal of fortune: Onyx**
   It's certainly a good time to look to a career change and for financial

Question: Is my partner having an affair?

We all have moments when we worry that our partner has found someone else. Unfortunately, sometimes this turns out to be true, but sometimes it's simply that we ourselves are feeling restless, and therefore we feel that our partner must be too! This kind of question about a third party simply reminds you why you are asking such a question in the first place. After all, we are seeking the truth about ourselves, not others.

1. **Crystal of illumination: Opal**
   You are in tune with others at the moment, but your imagination is over-active and your feelings are running high.
2. **Crystal of darkness: Amethyst**
   Could it be that your own desire for a passionate love life is simply distorting your mind?
3. **Crystal of fortune: Blue lace agate**
   Luckily, a friend will bring clarity and insight to the situation.

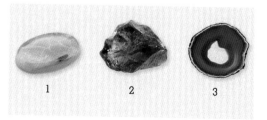

ZODIAC WHEEL CRYSTAL DIVINATION

Another fun method for crystal divination is to cast the crystals onto a zodiac wheel, as in the diagram below. You can either copy the circle onto a large piece of paper, or mark out the circle with a long piece of thread. The bigger you make the circle, the easier it is to use. I have often simply mapped out a circle on the smooth carpet on my floor of about two feet diameter.

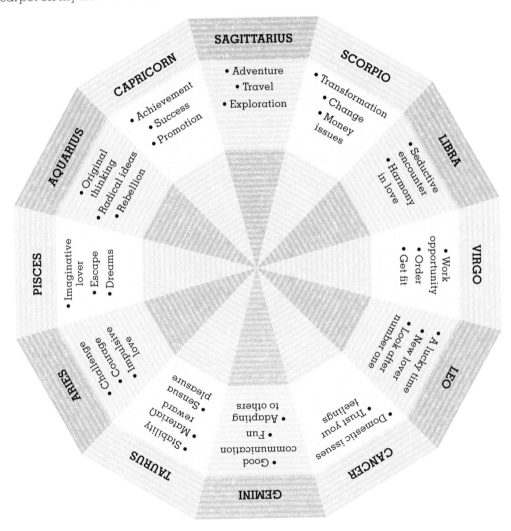

SAGITTARIUS
- Adventure
- Travel
- Exploration

SCORPIO
- Transformation
- Change
- Money issues

CAPRICORN
- Achievement
- Success
- Promotion

LIBRA
- Seductive encounter
- Harmony in love

AQUARIUS
- Original thinking
- Radical ideas
- Rebellion

VIRGO
- Work opportunity
- Order
- Get fit

PISCES
- Imaginative lover
- Escape
- Dreams

LEO
- A lucky time
- New lover
- Look after number one

ARIES
- Challenge
- Courage
- Impulsive love

CANCER
- Domestic issues
- Trust your feelings

TAURUS
- Stability
- Material reward
- Sensual pleasure

GEMINI
- Good communication
- Fun
- Adapting to others

DRAWING THE CRYSTALS

Place your crystals in a pouch or bag and gently stir them around with your hands until they are "shuffled." Sit in front of your zodiac wheel and focus on your specific question. For example, you might ask, "If I move to X will I be happy?"

Like the first reading you did, you are going to choose three crystals, in the following order: the crystal of illumination, the crystal of darkness, and the crystal of fortune. Pick a single crystal from the bag, and without glancing at it cast it gently onto the zodiac circle. This time, where the crystal falls in the circle is just as important as the crystal you choose. It's simply a matter of connecting ideas together, but if you find this too challenging to begin with, simply work with the spreads on pages 104–117 and later add the zodiac wheel associations as you gain more experience and practice.

EXAMPLE READING

1. **Crystal of illumination: Rose quartz**
   Lands on: Taurus
   Taurus is about material reward and stability. So the first crystal represents you now, both its quality as rose quartz (warm-hearted and wanting to be loved) and that you seek stability.
2. **Crystal of darkness: Onyx**
   Lands on: Leo
   If you look at the wheel, you'll see that Leo is about looking after oneself, and that onyx is about convention and structure. What could be the blockage here? That maybe you're trying too hard to stick to the tried and trusted?
3. **Crystal of fortune: Tiger's eye**
   Lands on: Scorpio
   This suggests that the outcome will be that with inspired thinking and courage you must make this change and move to X to be happy.

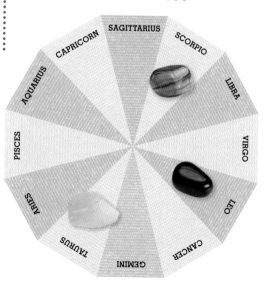

CRYSTAL ORACLES

The following interpretations give you a feel for the different energies behind the crystals, but also widen your interpretation to relate to the question you've asked. The crystal's vibrational energy will help you to draw on your own intuitive ability and it is that mystical center of yourself that reads and listens to the language coming from the universal storehouse of knowledge via the crystals.

RED CARNELIAN
⊶ Activate

Achievement is possible in most areas of your life right now, as long as you conquer any fears or self-doubt. Start making headway with your plans and your drive for success will pay off.

CITRINE
⊶ Communicate

This crystal enables you to transform negative thoughts into positive ones. You are about to make a good decision based on logic. Communication and all forms of travel are beneficial.

ROSE QUARTZ
⊶ Love

There is a chance for a wonderful rapport between you and someone special, or a love match is well favored. If single, you're about to meet someone who will change your life. All relationships can now improve.

MOONSTONE
⊶ Belonging

Intuition and feelings are powerful. It's time to go with what your heart truly wants. Take care you aren't being deceived by those who want to manipulate you. Family values may need reevaluating.

TIGER'S EYE
o—⊤ Inspire

A time when any new quest can be successfully completed, and a time to be different and show you have purpose and vision. Love relationships will be dramatic and challenging.

MALACHITE
o—⊤ Transform

A time for abundance, material rewards, or a strong sense of destiny. Also indicates that you can transform your life, as long as you stay awake to opportunity. Career success is coming your way.

PERIDOT
o—⊤ Discriminate

Discriminate with care and make sure you have all the evidence before making any decision. It's also time to spread your wings and interact with people who respect your individuality.

JADE
o—⊤ Harmony

A harmonious love life and success in romance. You are in harmony with the Universe, so manifest your desires; just take care you're not blind to the truth of someone's feelings for you.

TURQUOISE
o—⊤ Travel

Journeys are indicated, whether physical or intellectual. Explore new ideas, feel free of obligations, and you can now live life to the full. Love is boundless and you'll soon be free of past regrets.

OBSIDIAN
o—⊤ Materialize

The stone of manifestation. You can now ground your goals and improve all aspects of your lifestyle. If you have a vision, it's time to turn it into a reality. Persevere, and any challenges will be rewarded with a wonderful run of events.

AMBER

o—⚷ Rationalize

You have some radical plans and rebellious friends, but somehow you know that unconventional methods are going to work in your favor. Fight for your beliefs. They're the right ones.

OPAL

o—⚷ Sensitivity

You're acutely sensitive to other people's wishes, and feelings may be running high. Concentrate on your own beliefs and values, and remember you can't change things that cannot be changed.

AQUAMARINE

o—⚷ Romance

A stone of harmony and love. There will shortly be romance in the air. The tide is turning in your favor. Don't let other people's negativity stop you from doing what's best for you.

CLEAR QUARTZ CRYSTAL

o—⚷ Clarity

Your life will soon be filled with joy and a sense of personal success. You can now see clearly where you are going and why. Any difficult situations will soon be resolved and the air clear.

TOPAZ

o—⚷ Understanding

Decisions can be made and followed through with excellent results. Be more tolerant of other people and less judgmental, and it will bring you the results you're looking for.

TOURMALINE

o—⚷ Compassion

Friends are important to you now, and can give you good, objective advice. You will soon find true love, if you respect your own needs, or a lover is now ready to commit.

RED AGATE
○━━ Initiative

You can make progress in any work or relationship issue and resolve all problems. You must make it clear what you want, and why. A stranger brings unexpected but welcome ideas.

ORANGE CARNELIAN
○━━ Rebellion

Be innovative and promote some positive life changes. People may frustrate you but press ahead with your plans. Lovers may be radical, or refuse to play the game your way.

LAPIS LAZULI
○━━ Wisdom

The stone of wisdom indicates that you must use your head and not your heart. You can now forge ahead with career matters, educate yourself in new ideas, and widen your perspective. A global viewpoint will bring you success.

BLUE LACE AGATE
○━━ Vision

With imagination and vision, worldly success can be yours. Your idea can be made manifest, but don't sacrifice it for the sake of someone else.

ONYX
○━━ Structure

Organization, structure, and consistency are important qualities in your life now. You need a reliable set of rules to live by. But don't let material wealth matter to you more than love.

AMETHYST
○━━ Passion

A new romance or passionate love affair is indicated. If attached, it's timely to rekindle the romantic flames of your relationship. Sensually, you're in tune with your partner and you're about transform dull routines into passionate escapades.

INTRODUCING CRYSTAL SPREADS

So what are crystal spreads? These are simply a way of laying out the crystals in various patterns so that you can "read" one crystal at a time and also in relation to the question and other crystals in that spread.

The spread pattern itself is also symbolic, representing numbers or geometric shapes that have a deeper connection to the vibrational energy of the Universe. A crystal spread depends on two things. First, the position of the crystal, and second, the crystal's meaning or value related to that placement. Use the keyword or phrases of the interpretations given on the previous pages to help you read the spread.

On the following pages are some simple spreads to get you practicing; we then move onto relationship spreads (pages 108–109) and destiny spreads (110–117)— these are slightly longer than the previous ones, and will give you deeper insight into your choices and future plans. This is when you will begin to see that the crystals are reading you, as you are reading the crystals!

Spreads themselves are symbolic patterns often found in nature. They can also add value to your readings by connecting these patterns with numbers, crystals, and colors.

CRYSTALS AND NATURE

The best place to read crystals is actually out in the open—on a beach, in the garden or park, or some natural open space—simply because crystals are part of nature, and the more they are surrounded by natural elements without man-induced pollutants, the better they resonate to your readings. The time of year can be important too—readings during the waxing crescent moon cycle, as well as the summer solstice and spring equinox, will enhance the crystals' powers as they tune int o the changing solar energy.

If you do read your crystal spread indoors, place a cloth of silk scarf on the table or floor first, or place two white candles and incense such as sandalwood beside you, to help to enhance the vibrational quality of the stones.

Some of the best crystal work can be done outdoors, but as long as you are relaxed and in harmony with your surroundings, they can be done anywhere and at any time.

PREPARATIONS

Start your ritual either by lighting a candle or incense, or using a meditation technique. If you are outside, cast an imaginary circle of protection around you by pointing your finger in a huge circle as you turn three hundred and sixty degrees, first clockwise, then counterclockwise. This will protect you and your crystals and harmonize your own energy with that of the Universe. Alternatively, do the bubble of protection exercise on page 88.

WHAT DO I NEED?

Here is a simple spread to understand what you may be lacking in your life. This is divided into three different areas—love, career, and home. The two crystals for each area can be read independently or can be combined to give a deeper insightful answer. There are two levels of need: what you lack, or a gap in your life that you want to fill, and a need to give something back too—a hugely important part of working with the universal energy of crystals.

DRAWING THE CRYSTALS

Take a crystal one at a time from your pouch or bag, and place them in the order shown.

1. What I need in love
2. What I need in my career
3. What I need at home
4. What I need to give in love
5. What I need to give to my career
6. What I need to give at home

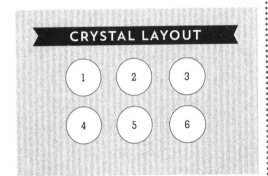

CRYSTAL LAYOUT

1 2 3

4 5 6

EXAMPLE READING

1. **Moonstone:** In love, I need to trust in my intuition.
2. **Jade:** In my career, I need some helpful mentors.
3. **Obsidian:** At home, I need to be more organized.
4. **Citrine:** What I need to give out in love is to open up and communicate my desires.
5. **Tiger's eye:** What I need to give to my career is inspirational ideas.
6. **Amethyst:** What I need to give at home is to put some passion into making it a lovely place to be.

WHAT DO I TRULY DESIRE?

This spread will sort out the things you really want in life right now, and the things you don't. Our moods change and so do our desires, so don't think that if you do this spread one day then the next day it will be the same. Remember that as your moods fluctuate, so the stones pick up on your energy.

DRAWING THE CRYSTALS

Pick five crystals one at a time from your pouch and lay them out in the order shown in the diagram.

1. My current mood
2. My future desire
3. My good influence
4. My difficult influence
5. The outcome

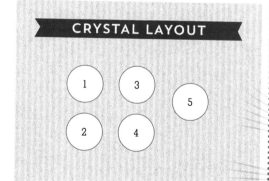

CRYSTAL LAYOUT

EXAMPLE READING

1. **Turquoise:** My current mood is restless and irresponsible.
2. **Amethyst:** My future desire is for a passionate love affair.
3. **Lapis lazuli:** If I widen my network or study a new subject, I'll meet up with the right kind of potential lover.
4. **Malachite:** I mustn't let materialistic or financial need cloud my judgment.
5. **Tourmaline:** An easygoing admirer will soon be charming me out of my restless mood.

FORTUNE SPREAD

This spread looks to the present and future to tell you where you are going in life. It also examines current and future outside influences, for good or not so good.

DRAWING THE CRYSTALS

Pick five crystals one at a time from your pouch and lay them out in the order shown in the diagram.

1. Me right now
2. Current influence
3. What I would love to become/do
4. Future influence
5. Where it will lead

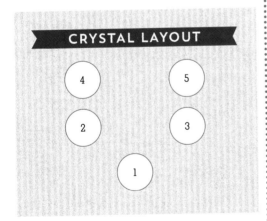

EXAMPLE READING

1. **Rose quartz:** I'm currently feeling quite romantic about someone and hoping that it will turn out to be a great relationship.
2. **Red carnelian:** The current influence is someone who thinks they know what's best for me, but they are just trying to manipulate me.
3. **Turquoise:** I would love to get some space from this influence and go traveling with my new romance.
4. **Peridot:** I will soon be able to interact with people who respect my individuality and personal viewpoint.
5. **Orange carnelian:** This will lead to some big changes and positive life choices.

THREE-LEVEL SELF

This spread looks at who you are on three levels: your intellectual self, your emotional self, and your spiritual self. There are two crystals for each self: the first describes the current energy and state of each self; the second describes how to improve or bestow happiness.

DRAWING THE CRYSTALS

Take one crystal at a time and place in the order shown in the diagram.

1. My intellectual self
2. My emotional self
3. My spiritual self
4. The crystal of mind improvement
5. The crystal of serenity and power
6. The crystal of spiritual happiness

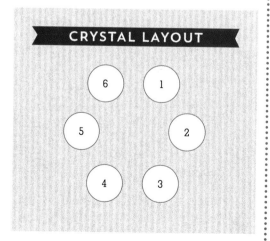

CRYSTAL LAYOUT

6   1
5   2
4   3

EXAMPLE READING

Here is an example reading, showing you how the last three crystals are actually the ones you will use to restore and promote good energy for all three sides of your self.

1. **Citrine:** I'm logical and decisive, so my mind is working well.
2. **Turquoise:** On the surface I'm fun-loving and happy, but I can't bear to make any decisions.
3. **Amber:** I'm ready to involve myself in deeper spiritual practice and have the vision to connect to higher planes of consciousness.
4. **Blue lace agate:** Although intellectually I'm in good spirits, I need to place blue lace agate in the northwest corner of my home to enhance imaginative thinking.
5. **Red agate:** To ensure I let out my feelings in the nicest possible way, I will wear or carry red agate. It will help me to show I mean business and prove to myself I'm not going to give in.
6. **Onyx:** I will keep a piece of onyx on my desk or table to act as a protective stone, as I am now working with my spiritual self and opening up to unknown energies.

THE COMPATIBILITY SPREAD

This is a useful spread to see how compatible you are with someone, whether a new friend, work colleague, or lover.

DRAWING THE CRYSTALS

Take five crystals one at a time from your pouch and lay them out in the order shown.

1. Me
2. The other person
3. Together now
4. Our mutual test
5. Our destiny together

CRYSTAL LAYOUT

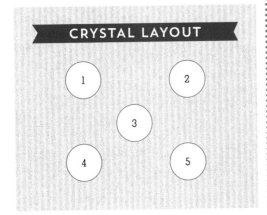

EXAMPLE READING

Question: I've recently been promoted at work, but a once-friendly colleague seems jealous. Can we still be friends?

1. **Red carnelian:** I'm feeling dynamic and full of spirit.
2. **Jade:** A colleague wants to be friends, but can't stop feeling bitter.
3. **Moonstone:** We are both intuitively aware of the other's feelings.
4. **Topaz:** If I tolerate their envy, I may win their support.
5. **Red agate:** Our destiny together is progressive, if we both start crusading for a mutual cause.

HOW YOU SEE EACH OTHER

This spread reveals how you and another person see each other, whether a love partner, a business colleague, or a family member. It is quite good fun to do it with the other person. However, if you do this alone, try not to project your own wishes or fears onto your partner's crystals!

DRAWING THE CRYSTALS

Decide beforehand whether you are going to be partner A or B in this diagram. Now draw the crystals one by one and place them as shown in the diagram.

1. How A sees B
2. How B sees A
3. What A wants from the relationship
4. What B wants from the relationship
5. Where A believes the relationship is going
6. Where B believes the relationship is going

CRYSTAL LAYOUT

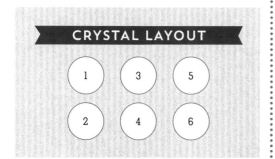

EXAMPLE READING

This is a reading between two first-time lovers.

1. **Clear quartz:** A sees B as joyful, goal-oriented, and clear-headed.
2. **Aquamarine:** B sees A as romantic, elusive, and a little unreliable.
3. **Topaz:** A wants the relationship to be open, free and easy, and non-judgmental.
4. **Obsidian:** B wants the relationship to be as solid as a, well, rock!
5. **Jade:** A believes the relationship will eventually be harmonious.
6. **Red carnelian:** B believes the relationship is going to need one of you to be the boss.

In this reading, we can see that A is positive about the relationship, but perhaps a little idealistic, while B is in need of security and needs motivation.

CHALLENGES AND OUTCOME

Throughout life we seem to be met by challenges and tests, and most of these are self-imposed. But they can become highly positive dynamics in our life. For example, we think we want to go and live in a different part of the country because "the grass looks greener" there. But actually, when we realize we're no better off moving, we feel let down by our own enthusiasm. This becomes more of a challenge, in that we are determined to prove that we can change our lifestyle. This is then a positive challenge, giving us a realistic outlook on our own expectations.

DRAWING THE CRYSTALS
1. Personal challenge right now
2. Relationship challenge right now
3. What is holding me back?
4. What motivates me?
5. Where will I get support?
6. What decision do I need to make?
7. The outcome

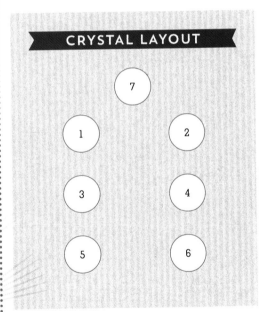

CRYSTAL LAYOUT

EXAMPLE READING

1. **Blue lace agate.** My personal challenge right now is to stick to my vision of what I want for the future, rather than be led astray by others. Alternatively, it may be that I am currently in need of a vision and have been denying that there is one calling me on.

2. **Amber:** My relationship challenge is that I need to rationalize decisions rather than dwelling on who is right and who is wrong.

3. **Onyx:** It seems that material wealth and stability are important to me, but it may be that I am so attached to that sense of security, it stops me fulfilling other dreams.

4. **Amethyst:** I am motivated by passion and power and that's what will wake me up to the truth.

5. **Orange carnelian:** My support will come from innovative ideas, which I can then develop into action.

6. **Tourmaline:** The decision I make will be to realize that I need to respect my own needs first.

7. **Topaz:** The outcome will be that with tolerance and care, I can sort out how to manifest my personal vision.

WHAT I NEED TO DISCOVER

As we carry on our life journey, we sometimes come across obstacles in our path, whether new ideas, different beliefs, or a total change of perspective. This bumpy ride can be hard, but this spread will help you to take some grand strides along the road. The three crystals for each theme can be read individually or preferably combined as I have shown in the example reading. This is also a chance to interpret whether the crystal is there to reinforce your positive qualities or to subdue any negative ones.

DRAWING THE CRYSTALS

As before, just take a crystal one at a time and lay them out in the order shown.

1, 2, 3 What I need to discover about love

4, 5, 6 What I need to discover about life

7, 8, 9 What I need to discover about my vocation

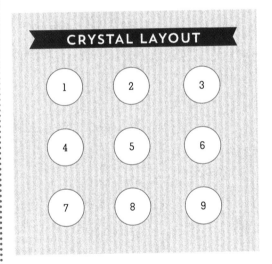

CRYSTAL LAYOUT

1   2   3

4   5   6

7   8   9

EXAMPLE READING

1. Rose quartz
2. Opal
3. Aquamarine

In love relationships I need to discover that sensual pleasure and romance are one thing (rose quartz) but I must accept that others are often more sensitive than they appear (opal). It may be that I now must make a few compromises and then harmony will return (aquamarine).

4. Clear quartz
5. Moonstone
6. Peridot

What I need to discover about life is that if I truly believe in myself, I can create personal happiness and a sense of self-belief will bring me creative rewards or gifts (clear quartz). I also need to be aware of family values (moonstone), even though I trust in my own first (peridot).

7. Turquoise
8. Citrine
9. Tiger's eye

What I need to discover in my vocation is that if I can expand my talents and skills (turquoise), that will lead me on to better things, and then I can fulfill my ambitions (citrine). It means daring to do something a little different, but in the risk I will find success (tiger's eye.)

THE ZODIAC YEAR

This time you're going to use twelve stones to represent each month of the year ahead. Each crystal will suggest the key theme that will be energized during the month. Obviously if you have a month where "romance" seems to be prominent, it's not necessarily the only month where romance will occur, but because it is highlighted, the crystal will work in your favor that month. Each month, carry or wear the highlighted crystal if you want to re-boost the positive benefits of its power.

DRAWING THE CRYSTALS

Lay down the crystals as shown in the diagram. Number one will be the month ahead, followed by the other eleven months in sequence. If you are doing the reading at the end of March, number one will be April and number twelve will be March—if it's the first week of March, March will be number one and April number twelve.

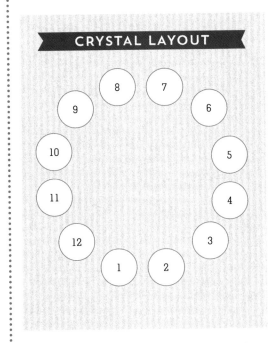

CRYSTAL LAYOUT

EXAMPLE READING

1. **Jade:** Well-being and happiness are indicated. You will be perfect in all you do.

2. **Rose quartz:** Love and romance are around every corner. You will discover people love you for who you truly are.

3. **Obsidian:** A challenging month, but persevere with your ambitions and don't give in to self-doubt; you will succeed.

4. **Moonstone:** Use your intuition, follow your hunches, trust your inner guide, focus on all aspects of your spiritual well-being, and you will feel great too.

5. **Bloodstone:** Your integrity and confidence come to the fore and you could be up for a new position in your career.

6. **Agate:** A prosperous month when material benefits could put a smile on your face.

7. **Citrine:** Speak your mind, but avoid tactlessness; this is a great month to transmit ideas and communicate the truth.

8. **Red carnelian:** Your sensual needs are met and looking after number one takes precedence.

9. **Amethyst:** A passionate change of heart, but you're going to find it's exactly what you have always wanted.

10. **Lapis lazuli:** People can offer you great advice and good ideas. You can now forge ahead with career matters.

11. **Malachite:** Prosperous month, when all that you do or say seems to work in your favor.

12. **Turquoise:** A well-earned break is called for; travel is favored, and love too.

FUTURE DESIRES

This is a little different from all the other spreads as the first five crystals you must choose yourself. Place all your crystals out on the table and after focusing on them for a few minutes, take five crystals that "speak" to you, or that you simply prefer to work with right now—but they must be relevant to your future desires from the list given below. Do think clearly about which stones you choose and ensure that they represent (whether by color or symbol) the particular desire or wish. Then choose the last five crystals at random and place them next to the desire stones—the second stone will show you how to make those wishes come true.

DRAWING THE CRYSTALS

1. My ideal future is…
2. Where I want to be this time next year
3. What I want to achieve
4. What I want to let go of
5. What I want to learn

CRYSTAL LAYOUT

1a	1b
2a	2b
3a	3b
4a	4b
5a	5b

KEYNOTE

There are many other spreads you can create to use with crystals, either by adapting popular tarot card spreads you can find in books or on the Internet, or simply by making up your own geometric patterns and designs.

EXAMPLE READING

1. My ideal future is…
1a. My chosen stone: Malachite
This represents prosperity, ambition, and success.
1b. Randomly selected stone: Citrine
I can make this wish come true if I network, communicate with people I don't know, focus on my goals, and make decisions based on logic and objective thinking.

2. Where I want to be this time next year
2a. My chosen stone: Orange carnelian
To have made some innovative changes to my lifestyle.
2b. Randomly selected stone: Turquoise
Through travel and adventure I will find the right way to make these changes.

3. What I want to achieve
3a. My chosen stone: Onyx
An organized and materially successful business.
3b. Randomly selected stone: Topaz
If I am tolerant of others, I will get their help to succeed.

4. What I need to let go of
4a. My chosen stone: Amber
My radical and often careless way of behaving.
4b. Randomly selected stone: Opal
I will begin to understand myself better if I concentrate on finding out what really matters to me.

5. What I want to learn
5a. My chosen stone: Lapis lazuli
To be wiser, more rational, and to become an expert in my chosen field.
5b. Randomly selected stone: Clear quartz crystal
I will at last be able to see where I am going and why.

1a   1b

2a   2b

3a   3b

4a   4b

5a   5b

CRYSTALS AND TAROT PROGRAMMING

One of the most potent and practical uses of divining with crystals is when you combine them with a corresponding tarot card to infuse the crystal with the power of the archetype associated with the card.

This energizes and programs the crystal for a short-term or permanent effect—usually until you "clear" the energy from the crystal in a reverse ritual (see page 23). It's rather like when you hold the crystal in your hand to draw on its energy or to give out your own. The tarot archetype is drawn into the crystal so that when you wear or carry it, you are also carrying the tarot card's psychic blueprint.

The Major Arcana are the twenty-two cards of the deck numbered one to twenty-one, and the Fool, which is unnumbered. Each card is associated with one of the twenty-two crystals that we have been using so far, and also by association to planets and zodiac signs.

Tarot cards are a powerful way to program your crystals with specific archetypal energy.

TAROT PROGRAMMING

Take a while to look through your tarot cards and crystals, and think about which "speak to you" or seem to respond well to your specific desire or need, and also which can be used successfully in your quest.

1. Once you have decided which crystal and which card are most appropriate for your purpose (see their Tarot Associations and Energies table on the next page), place the crystal and card (face up) on a table in front of you and sit quietly for a moment. Acknowledge that your chosen purpose is for the benefit of all. Maybe you are seeking new romance, in which case you would probably choose the Lovers tarot card to empower your crystal with potent love. The crystal traditionally associated with the Lovers is citrine; however, if you prefer, you could use a favorite stone such as rose quartz or white quartz—it is entirely up to you to decide which stone feels "right" for your purpose.

2. Next, place the crystal on top of the card and repeat the card's name three times (for example, "the Lovers, the Lovers, the Lovers") and ask for the energy of the card to empower the crystal.

3. Now say aloud what the specific purpose is. For example, "I want to find new love/romance."

4. Carry the crystal with you wherever you go and soon you will find new love—often when you least expect it.

VI

THE LOVERS

TAROT ASSOCIATIONS AND ENERGIES

Here is a brief guide to each tarot card's energy and benefits, its traditionally associated crystals and their brief programming keyword. So, for example, if you wanted to program your crystal for sexual vitality, or physical attraction, you'd program the crystal with the power of the Devil. Using the Devil's traditional associated crystal, obsidian, would amplify this energy and create an aura of sexual magic around you.

TAROT ASSOCIATIONS AND ENERGIES

TAROT CARD	ASSOCIATED CRYSTAL	KEYWORD	ENERGIES AND BENEFITS
The Fool	Bloodstone	Rebellion	Embarking on short journeys, exploring the world, feeling free and spirited
The Magician	Topaz	Wisdom	Focus, intellectual ability, insight, manifestation, magic
The High Priestess	Selenite	Sensitivity	Clairvoyance, psychic energy, inner guidance, spiritual understanding
The Empress	Pink tourmaline	Compassion	Nurturing, grounding, creativity, new life, successful birth
The Emperor	Red carnelian	Action	Authority, asserting oneself, new projects
The Hierophant	Rose quartz	Value	Transmitting ideas, teaching, finding mentors
The Lovers	Citrine	Connection	Love relationships, romance, making decisions, harmony
The Chariot	Aquamarine	Vision	Taking control of your destiny, knowing where you are going

TAROT CARD	ASSOCIATED CRYSTAL	KEYWORD	ENERGIES AND BENEFITS
Strength	Tiger's eye	Inspiration	Self-confidence, courage, determination, goal-seeking
The Hermit	Peridot	Discrimination	Patience, inner peace, spiritual enlightenment
The Wheel of Fortune	Lapis lazuli	Knowledge	Inspiration, taking chances, being lucky, impulsive choices
Justice	Jade	Harmony	Clarity, beneficial legal or financial affairs, agreements, compromises
The Hanged Man	Blue lace agate	Sacrifice	Mystical empowerment, seeing the truth, giving up bad habits
Death	Malachite	Transformation	Transformation, new beginnings, dumping emotional baggage
Temperance	Turquoise	Going with the flow	Harmonious relationships, freedom and commitment, self-belief
The Devil	Obsidian	Integrity	Sexual attraction, physical vitality
The Tower	Agate	Progression	Breaking bad habits, emotional breakthrough, healing old wounds
The Star	Amber	Realization	Intellectual wisdom, spiritual insight, meditation, creative inspiration
The Moon	Moonstone	Intuition	Dream work, keeping secrets, deeper understanding, magical love
The Sun	Clear quartz	Optimism	Discovering the truth, success, happiness, long-term commitment
Judgment	Amethyst	Awakening	Fresh perspective, transitions, consolidation, acceptance
The World	Onyx	Structure	Long journeys, completion, fulfillment, integration

DOWSING WITH A CRYSTAL PENDULUM

Pendulum dowsing has been used for thousands of years to find lost objects, determine the sex of an unborn child, or to choose dates for special events. In ancient Egypt it was used to decide on the best place to grow crops. Pendulums have also been used to find underground tunnels, water courses, hidden mines, and lines of geopathic stress.

Crystal dowsing is simply about enabling the universal energy to channel through you and the crystals as you work in tandem.

Crystal dowsing uses a crystal suspended from (usually) a fine chain which you hold out in front of you when asking questions or looking for guidance. The pendulum swings (including when it doesn't move at all) determine a possible five responses. You can use a crystal pendulum to make decisions, select a potential partner, ask yes/no questions about the future, locate lost objects, or evaluate a situation or person.

CHOOSING A PENDULUM

Crystal pendulums all have their own unique vibrations, and there are many available today. Choose one that you like the look of, or is a favorite crystal of yours. You should select one that you like the weight of, and it should be able to swing widely and perfectly when held between the finger and thumb. Round, cylindrical, or spherical shapes are best because they swing symmetrically.

HOW DOES IT WORK?

Universal energy permeates everything, flowing through the earth and through you. As you hold the pendulum and ask the Universe a question, it is the tiny involuntary movements of your hand and the crystal's vibrational electromagnetic field in reaction to the universal energy, known as the "ideomotor" response, that cause it to swing. The crystal is working with the universal knowledge deep within you. The answer comes from this energy via your unconscious. The best results come when you are totally objective.

LETTING GO

In this exercise, you're going to learn how to let go of your own mind's desires and intentions when dowsing, so that what you want to happen or think you know doesn't lead you to unconsciously control the swings of the pendulum to achieve those outcomes.

1. Take your chosen crystal pendulum and let it hang from between your finger and thumb with your elbow resting on a table. It doesn't matter if it swings or not, nor at the moment in which direction. Just gaze at the crystal for a few seconds and consciously think about its shape, color, and associated symbols.

2. Focus on these three qualities, until no other thought enters your head, just its color, shape, and meaning. Keep focusing on this until it becomes a pattern of words in your mind, a mantra of reflection.

3. Close your eyes and continue focusing on the words for another minute. Now stop thinking of these words, open your eyes, and your mind will be empty for a few seconds, maybe longer. These moments of emptiness are when you have let go of all the chatter in your head to give you a brief view into the deeper unconsciousness of yourself, where all is calm. Once you find this place, go back to it each time you begin to dowse with your pendulum.

SWINGS AND ROUNDABOUTS

Here is a step-by-step guide to using a crystal to dowse, whether to find missing objects or to have yes or no answers to specific questions.

The pendulum can only swing in four possible ways, but it can also just appear to stand still without moving.

1. It can swing from side to side or in a "perpendicular" way.
2. It can swing in an up or down or in a "vertical" way.
3. It can swing in an elliptical or circular motion in a clockwise direction.
4. It can swing in an elliptical or circular motion in an counterclockwise direction.

Crystal pendulums all have their own unique vibrations.

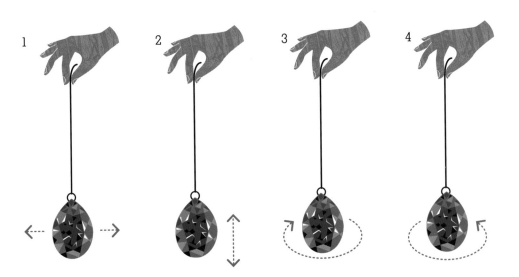

ASSIGNING PENDULUM SWINGS

With this knowledge you now have to define what each swing signifies: one swing for "yes," one for "no," one for "don't know," and one for "try again." Swings and corresponding answers are not the same for everyone. Some people may get an up and down swing for "yes," while another person will get a clockwise circular motion. This is according to your personal vibrational energy which connects you to the Universe via the crystal.

1. Hold the pendulum over an object to which you know the answer is "yes." For example, if you hold your pendulum over a table, and ask, "Is this a table?", then whichever swing takes precedence is your personal swing, which will always give the answer "yes." (However, this may change from time to time, so it's worth checking your swing responses about every few months as the energy vibrations of the Universe and the crystal can change with your own developing psychic energy.)

2. Check it again by asking another question you know the answer to. If you're female, ask, "Am I a female?" and so on.

3. Next, check your "no" swings by holding the pendulum over an object to which you know the answer will be "no." For example, hold the pendulum over the table again and ask, "Is this a book?" The swing should now change to another movement. But if you find this doesn't work, and the crystal swings in the same direction, then you may not yet be confident enough in your ability. Simply repeat one of the first exercises for the crystal's power to re-establish your own link to your stone.

For an "ask again" or a "don't know" answer you must define which of the other two swings is which.

4. Next you can move on to asking questions to which you don't know the answers. Once the responses are embedded in your unconscious (the link to both the pendulum and vibrational harmony in the Universe), you can then trust the response, whatever it is.

CRYSTAL DOWSING EXAMPLES

On the following pages there are four different examples of situations in which you can use a crystal pendulum.

FINDING A LOST OBJECT

One of the most common and fun ways to use a crystal pendulum is to find a lost object. When we lose something, like a bunch of keys, a ring, a watch, or wallet, we have usually simply misplaced them or forgotten where we put them, but it can create an awful lot of anxiety. By using a crystal pendulum to find the object, you won't be panicking about where it is or whether it has disappeared from your sight forever. Perform the following test to practice.

1. Ask a friend to hide the object somewhere in your home while you step outside for ten minutes. You really mustn't have any clue where they are going to place it.

2. Stay calm and relaxed, and prepare your pendulum. The questions are all going to be yes or no answers, so make them as clear as possible. To get you off to a good start, try one that you already know the answer to: "Is the object in my home?" This also checks that the pendulum is swinging to your preferred "yes" swing. A positive response will give you belief in the answers too.

3. Now narrow down the search by asking, "Is the object in the bathroom?" Go through each room in the house until you get a positive response. Then you can ask specific questions like, "Is it under the bed?" or "Is the object in the dishwasher?", and so on. By the time you get this far, you may well see the object, or the pendulum will start to show positive results over a rug or a chest of drawers. Have fun!

HARMONIOUS DATING

This is a slightly different way to use the crystal pendulum. It doesn't rely on your positive or negative swings; rather, its own harmonic vibrations concerning you and another person will reveal whether you are compatible or have a good affinity. When you first meet someone, it can sometimes be difficult to know if you're going to get along with that person or not, even if you fancy them or have agreed on a first date. To find out in advance whether this relationship will be harmonious or not, try the following.

1. Find two crystals of roughly a similar size and color—red crystals like garnet or ruby are especially potent for love compatibility. Place them on a table with a gap of about six inches between them. Suspend your dowsing crystal midway between the two stones, and after a few moments the pendulum should start to swing from side to side—as if moving from one crystal to another. This means they are in harmony with each other, whether or not your personal positive response is this swing or not. Obviously, two red crystals are compatible: they have the same color, symbol, and similar energies.

2. Now replace one of the crystals with a very different object, such as a watch, a pen, or a coin. Suspend the crystal again halfway between the two objects, and this time you'll see that it either stands still, or the swing moves up and down (backwards and forwards), avoiding the two objects. This means the objects are not in harmony.

3. You can now apply this to you and your first date (or any encounter that is relevant).

4. Write your name on a small piece of paper, and on another piece of paper, write your date's name. Place them on the table as you did the two crystals. Suspend the crystal halfway between them and see what happens. If it moves from one name to another, then you can expect a harmonious date; if its stays still or moves up and down, then you can expect a difficult first date. However, it may be that the tension and challenge of the unknown proves to be more enticing than easy compatibility.

DESIRABLE LIST

The crystal pendulum can also be used to help you achieve a desire or goal. The great thing about the pendulum is that it will help you to sort out which goals and desires are genuinely right for you or realistically attainable, and which may be totally impossible.

1. First, write down a list of all the things you long for or desire, even if they sound like pipe dreams—write each wish on a separate piece of paper. For example:

> • *I want to marry a millionaire*
>
> • *I long to travel the world*
>
> • *I wish I could change my hairstyle*
>
> • *I long for new romance*
>
> • *I want to be healthy and wise*
>
> • *I wish I had a family*
>
> • *I wish I lived in a French chateau*

2. As you can see, some of these wishes sound highly unlikely, but to the one wishing for them, they are, of course, as desirable as the ones that are easily remedied.

3. Now lay your desires out in a row, with your greatest desire first, and so on.

4. Suspend your pendulum over the first desire. Close your eyes and think about it for a while. Is this a life-changing wish? Would you still be able to be yourself? Would other people like you more or less, or would there be no change? Now open your eyes and watch the response of your pendulum. Obviously, if it gives a positive swing, then this is a good desire to follow up; if it gives a negative swing, it indicates that this is something that is not attainable right now. (But you can always try again in the future!)

5. Suspend the pendulum over each piece of paper and make notes of the responses. Whichever wishes the pendulum makes positive swings over, separate those from the don't knows and the negatives, and concentrate on these goals. Over the next few days whittle the desires down to one wish with your pendulum, and affirm to the Universe that you will attempt from now on to achieve this goal. Through the pendulum your unconscious mind is in tune with the universal energy—this is now to your benefit to manifest your dream.

MY POTENTIAL

Finally, you can always ask the pendulum to reveal things about yourself that you may find it hard to be objective about. However, this also depends on whether you are consciously making the pendulum swing in the way you want it to or not. This divination exercise will require complete objectivity and a fair degree of openness and self-acceptance before you begin.

1. Find a quiet place to sit with your pendulum and relax. Clear your mind of any negative thoughts and perform the Letting Go exercise on page 123. Say the following test statements out loud one at a time:

> • *I love myself*
>
> • *I love the Universe and am part of the whole*
>
> • *I am a good friend*
>
> • *I am willing to help anyone*
>
> • *I do not judge others*
>
> • *I don't have any inhibitions*
>
> • *I enjoy my own company*
>
> • *I'm happy being single/attached*

2. Close your eyes and repeat the first statement a few times in your head, then watch your pendulum. If it gives a positive swing, you're in tune with this aspect of yourself; if it gives a negative swing, then you need to work on this area. If you get an indecisive response, then it is most likely that you are not comfortable with the statement and need to work on this area. Repeat this process for each statement on the list.

CHAPTER FOUR

THE KEY
to
CRYSTALS
& HEALING

○━ Crystals help to restore
balance to the chakras

○━ Carry certain stones with you
to promote well-being

○━ Use crystals for psychological
and emotional healing

○━ Develop your spiritual link to the
Universe with crystals

CRYSTALS AND HEALING

This final chapter will enable you to work with crystals for healing or restoring imbalances in your emotional and spiritual self, as well as for general life enhancement.

On the following pages you will find exercises on working with crystals and the chakras and how to balance these important invisible energy centers around your body. You can then move on to working with crystals to balance and bring harmony to all aspects of your life: for psychological and emotional healing, for spiritual development, and for life enhancement.

Please do remember that healing crystals are not medical prescriptions and are not cures; they simply help in the process of self-understanding and enhancement of your own unique healing powers.

PREPARING THE MIND

Before you begin any spiritual healing work, you must be able to enter into a state of complete calm and repose. The meditation ritual on the following pages will help you. Once you've tried the meditation technique, practice it on a daily basis if you can. It's not only a great warm-up for crystal work, it's also a great way to leave stress behind, to energize your mind, body, and spirit, and it even has the effect of helping to lower blood pressure and to calm you in a gentle, natural way.

When you first start working with crystals for healing, you will find that by meditating before you start any ritual, you are already in the right frame of mind, and you can connect more easily to the Universe and the vibrational energies of the crystals.

MEDITATION RITUAL

1. Find a comfortable place to sit where you won't be disturbed.

2. Take your favorite meditational crystal in your hand and close your eyes. (The best for meditation are selenite and amethyst, but use whatever you feel is right for you.) First of all take a few deep, long breaths and then begin to concentrate on your eyelids, and how when they are closed, they are filled with warmth and a glow of light. They are already calming your mind.

3. Turn your attention to the crystal in your hand. Imagine its color permeating the skin of your hand, its light and power softening all your muscles, tendons, and joints. Now this warm, colored energy moves on up through your hand. Feel the color of the crystal beginning to fill every pore of your body with its warmth and universal light. You feel your body gradually softening, your spine relaxed but still straight. You feel warm, calm, and peaceful.

4. With your eyes still closed, start to concentrate on your breathing. Your breathing will calm you down to a quiet, peaceful state, and fill you with healing, positive energy. Your in-breath will fill you with clear, purifying oxygen. Your out-breath removes all tensions. If you find you can't focus on your breathing for long, then gently bring your attention back to it again. As you develop more awareness of your power, you will find it easier to relax, your breathing will become deeper, and you will soon arrive at the silent, still place.

5. If you find you're distracted by other thoughts, let them pass you by, as if they were clouds in the sky. Let them pass through your mind, they are simply thoughts, nothing more.

6. Now focus your attention in your mind on an image of your crystal. Notice the color of the stone, the texture of the surface. Is it rough or smooth? Is it cold or hot, sharp or shiny? Be aware of its size, color, and shape. See its every detail and then see it as a whole. This focus will help you to stay in the moment. Keep focusing, keep thinking of the crystal in your mind.

7. As you concentrate on the crystal, you will discover another part of your mind that becomes aware of that very concentration.

8. You may also become aware of distractions. Be aware of these things, but don't be put off concentrating on the crystal. Keep turning your attention back to the image of the crystal. Now, slowly let the image of the crystal fade away. It is as if the colors are fading into nothing and you see only a vague, misty crystal, and then it's gone from view and there is nothing in your mind. There is no image, no sound, no thought, there is nothing. Now you will find yourself in the silent place, even if only for a few minutes.

9. Here in this still, empty place, you can rest for a while.

10. When you are ready, open your eyes and gaze for a few moments at your crystal and thank it for the power it has given you. Then place it in a safe place until you use the ritual again.

CHAKRAS AND CRYSTALS

Eastern spiritual traditions maintain that universal energy, known as "prana" in India, and "chi" in Chinese philosophy, flows through the body, linked by seven subtle energy centers known as chakras. The word chakra is a Sanskrit word meaning "wheel."

These energies constantly revolve or spiral around and through our bodies in a vertical direction vibrating at different frequencies. They correspond to the energy of seven colors, which are traditionally associated with seven spiritual gemstones. These stones invoke powerful healing energies and restore the chakra balance.

As we've already seen, crystals respond to the electromagnetic charge that is coursing through our bodies. If our chakra energy is underactive, the vibration of the stones will help to harmonize, balance, and stimulate these energies; similarly, if the energy is overactive, certain stones will help to subdue it. When stones are worn or carried on the body, or placed on the specific chakra centers for healing purposes, they stimulate the corresponding chakra so that both personal spiritual and physical power is restored.

Each chakra is aligned with one of the seven vibrational colors of the spectrum of the rainbow, which by turn connect to the crystal color energies. By wearing specific gemstones for each chakra, you can increase your energy levels and enhance spiritual harmony. The chakra colors are: red, orange, yellow, green, blue, indigo, and violet. If the chakras are not balanced, or if the energies are blocked, you may find you have negative thoughts or are physically tired or depressed. When the chakras are functioning normally, each will automatically respond to the particular energies needed from the universal energy field. Crystals vibrate at the correct spectrum frequency, and therefore help to activate the right kind of energy. There are also seven stones that can subdue chakra energy when the chakra is overactive. The fourteen stones are listed on pages 142–145.

AWAKENING THE CHAKRAS

Crystals are often placed on chakra spots to aid in either reinforcing or subduing the energy, but this is usually done by a skilled practitioner while the subject is lying down. However, you can hold, wear, and carry specific stones for the same purpose.

It's important to know or have a sense of the state of your own chakras. Use the exercise on the page opposite to help you understand these threshold energies, to increase your awareness of how to open up to their empowering energy, and to close them down when you've finished working with them.

THE THIRD EYE CHAKRA

If we think about color, we can see how the lightest crystals seem to resonate to the higher planes of consciousness; white and clear crystals, as we have seen, are about clarity and vision, while blue stones resonate to the psychic realm. As they become more violet or purple, they also vibrate to a higher ultraviolet frequency, where white and violet are at the spiritual chakra end of our experience. So, when we attempt to connect to the third eye, or even to the crown chakra, we can use stones such as diamonds, amethysts, clear quartz, or topaz.

AWAKENING THE THIRD EYE CHAKRA

1. Take a piece of amethyst and clear quartz roughly the same shape and size and place them on a table in front of you.

2. Close your eyes, take one in each hand and shuffle them between your hands until (unless you're cheating!) you don't know which stone is in which hand. This may take a while, but really make it clear to yourself and your mind that you don't know which stone is which. If the stones are a very different shape or size, then do this exercise with two photos or images cut to the same shape and size.

3. Now place one piece of paper or stone against the middle of your brow. What does it feel like? What sense or feeling do you get? Place it back on the table.

4. Next, take up the other stone or piece of paper, and do the same thing. Take a while to feel or sense these experiences.

5. Then, with eyes still closed, try to imagine the two stones side by side and intuit which one is which. Open your eyes and see if you were right. If you get it wrong, it's likely you need to spend more time working with stones to help you boost your spiritual powers.

CHAKRA AWAKENING

Most of us don't even think about our chakra energy, let alone how to sense or feel it. This exercise will bring you closer to understanding this powerful healing energy.

1. Sit on the ground or somewhere comfortable, preferably cross-legged. Do the meditation technique on pages 136–137 to calm your mind and get into a relaxed and open state.

2. Start with your root chakra. Move your hands to the base of your spine with your palms facing inwards, without touching your body. Hold your hands about one to two inches away from your lower back. You should feel the energy radiating from this chakra. It may feel warm and solid if it's in good condition; if it's cold or feels floppy, then you may need to empower it by carrying the appropriate crystal.

3. Next, move your hands slowly round to the front of your body and up to the sacral chakra. Hold your hands lightly together with fingers touching in a slight cupping shape, with no gaps. With palms facing your belly, keep your hands still and begin to sense how this chakra feels. Is it watery or does it feel like a gentle flow of energy? (Indicating the fact that it governs the urinary and reproductive system.)

4. Now move your hands up to your solar plexus region, which usually feels warmer and often fiery, governing the pancreas, liver, and nervous system.

5. Move your hands up to the heart chakra, where there is lightness and mobility, governing the thymus gland and circulation. Keep aware of these different areas and your personal reactions to them, not just through your hands but through your sixth sense.

6. Next, move your hands up to the throat chakra and then the third eye chakra. The throat governs communication, the third eye, intuition. What does this feel like in your own words?

7. Finally, at the crown chakra hold your hands above your head and feel the energy buzzing and radiating from the area concerned with your higher or spiritual self.

8. Place your hands back down in your lap. All the chakras have been refreshed and awoken by your awareness of them. Close your eyes and now imagine closing down each chakra as if you were closing a pair of window shutters to guard and save the energy.

REINFORCING STONES

When your chakra energy is weak or not functioning as it should, these crystals will help to stimulate and balance your well-being.

GARNET

CHAKRA: Root

Red garnets were favored in Greek and Roman antiquity and became known for their power to stimulate business success and career goals. Placing three or more garnets on your desk will help you to achieve your professional aims. When worn as jewelry, garnets aid popularity and self-esteem, and bring a sense of spiritual understanding and empathy to emotional relationships.

RUBY

CHAKRA: Sacral

The ancient Chinese Taoists considered the ruby to be the stone of fertility and virility. They were laid beneath the foundation of ancient Chinese and East Asian buildings to secure good fortune to the structure. Rubies empower you with financial know-how and make you feel good to be you. The ruby makes you realize that you have an individual purpose and destiny.

TOPAZ

CHAKRA: Solar plexus

Topaz enhances imagination and activates the law of attraction. Topaz is used to invoke faith and belief in one's spiritual quest, and is also a great stone for artists, fashion designers, architects, writers, decorators, or anyone who needs to boost their creativity. The most famous topaz, known as the "Braganza diamond," set in the Portuguese crown jewels, is colorless, and was originally thought to be a diamond.

PINK TOURMALINE

CHAKRA: Heart

According to an old Egyptian legend, tourmaline, on its long journey up from the center of the Earth, passed over a rainbow. In doing so, it assumed all the colors of the spectrum, and is still often called the "gemstone of the rainbow." The name tourmaline comes from the Singhalese words *"tura mali"* or *"stone with mixed colors."* Pink tourmaline is the most important for spiritual work and symbolizes compassion, love, warmth, and empathy.

AMETHYST

CHAKRA: Third eye

The true stone of spiritual healing and enlightenment, the amethyst is often used by mystics, psychics, healers, and religious leaders for its intuitive, transcendent, and spiritually awakening properties. Its calming influence on the mind makes the wearer kind and gentle. It also promotes peace, love, courage, protection against thieves, and happiness.

SAPPHIRE

CHAKRA: Throat

An old myth says that the Ten Commandments given to Moses were written on tablets of sapphire. The sapphire's spiritual powers of communication evoke in the wearer an ability to be enlightened by divine wisdom and, on a more worldly level, to communicate effectively. Empowering the wearer with spiritual enlightenment and inner peace, the sapphire is believed to boost psychic powers such as psychokinesis, telepathy, clairvoyance, and astral projection.

DIAMOND

CHAKRA: Crown

Diamonds are made from the same elements as the stars and galaxies. They help us to connect not only to the cosmos, but to our own true power, strength, and autonomy. A symbol of purity and fidelity, the diamond also brings love and clarity to relationships and creates long-term bonds. Diamonds are also energy amplifiers. So negative thoughts will be even more negative when wearing a diamond!

SUBDUING STONES

When our chakras are out of balance because they are overactive, this often manifests in our behavior toward others. These crystals will subdue and restore balance to your moods.

BLACK TOURMALINE
CHAKRA: Root

Brought to Europe by Dutch traders in the eighteenth century, tourmaline was known as the "ash puller," because it was believed that when laid near burning coals for a long time it had the power to attract and then repel the hot ashes. Black tourmaline gives one a sense of grounding, security, and personal power.

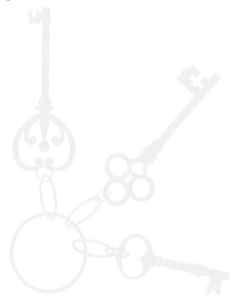

JADE
CHAKRA: Sacral

Jade talismans and amulets have been worn in the Far East since the fourth century BCE. Jade amulets are still highly popular, and jade statues, jewelry, and carved figures are often given to family, lovers, and friends for protection. Jade calms, invokes new romance, self-love and tolerance, and increases trustworthiness and fidelity.

AMBER
CHAKRA: Solar plexus

When transparent, this fossilized tree resin often reveals tiny insects trapped inside. Thought to draw all forms of disease from the body, amber lightens the mind, removes negative thoughts, and imbues the body with vitality. It also encourages self-expression, patience, and creativity.

MALACHITE

CHAKRA: Heart

Thought by the ancient Egyptians to invoke power and sagacity, malachite was once used to line the inside of the pharaoh's headdress in the hope that he would rule wisely. Malachite is also believed to give us the ability to be true to ourselves in relationship to the world, and yet to stay in balance with it.

TURQUOISE

CHAKRA: Throat

The word turquoise comes from the French "pierre turquoise," meaning "Turkish stone." This dates to the early Renaissance when European traders and wealthy Venetian merchants often purchased the stones in Turkish bazaars. Thought to be a talisman of luck, success, ambition, and creativity, the stone protects, purifies, and enables the wearer to see and communicate clearly.

OPAL

CHAKRA: Crown

In Greek mythology, opals were believed to be Zeus's tears of joy after the victory over the Titans. The stone is said to center and concentrate the mind, promoting happy dreams, optimism, enthusiasm, and creativity. It is also used to release inhibitions and to inspire love and passion.

LAPIS LAZULI

CHAKRA: Third eye

The ancient Egyptians prized this stone, believing the gold flecks were fragments of the stars in the sky, or of the gods themselves. Even the robes of priests or royalty were dyed with lapis (ground down to form an incredible dark blue pigment) to indicate their divine status. Today, lapis is worn to help the wearer to accept the truth, and to bring objectivity and clarity.

THE CHAKRA ENERGIES

We now look at each chakra in turn and how to work out if you need to reinforce its power or subdue it, depending on your psychological traits. Be as honest with yourself as you can be, and then the crystals will work honestly with you.

1. THE BASE OR ROOT CHAKRA

The base chakra is located at the base of the spine, centered between the last disc of the spine and the pubic bone to the front. This chakra is concerned with our sense of being grounded. It provides a firm base and sense of security, plus it controls the basic functions of the body. If you have a feeble base chakra, you'll feel spaced out and not in touch with the world, or you may feel threatened by other people and unable to get any project under way.

The base chakra is associated with red, and is energized by wearing or carrying a garnet. This stone will enhance your sense of security, release you from fears and self-doubt, and enable you to trust in yourself and others. If you are too dominating, pushy, and angry at the world, then to subdue this energy, use black tourmaline.

2. THE SACRAL CHAKRA

Located approximately a hand's breadth below the navel, the sacral chakra is concerned with your sex drive, creativity, and emotional state. It vibrates to the color orange. If this chakra is underactive, you'll have little confidence in your sexuality and will fear getting close to anyone. You may have problems relating to other people and fear they just want you as a sexual object. You may be emotionally manipulative and have very low self-esteem.

By wearing or carrying ruby, you will enhance your ability to flow with your emotions freely and to reach out to others, both sexually and creatively. If your sacral chakra is overactive, you may have a seductive character, be promiscuous, or demand too much from others. To calm down this overactive chakra, wear or carry jade.

3. THE SOLAR PLEXUS CHAKRA

Situated between the navel and the breastbone, the third chakra relates to the color yellow and is the seat of personal power. Rather like having one's own inner sun, it gives us a strong ego, a sense of our personal character, individuality, and willpower. If this chakra isn't shining, then we let others dominate us, feel afraid to express our personal opinion, or worry about what others will think about us. If we have too much of this chakra, we're bossy, careless, egotistic, and too proud for our own good.

To calm this overactive chakra, wear or carry amber. To boost this chakra, wear or carry topaz. This will restore your outgoing nature and give you more self-respect and expressiveness. You will enjoy taking on new challenges and have a strong sense of personal power.

HARA

Just a few inches below your belly button, and just above the sacral chakra, lies what is known as the "Hara." This is an invisible energy center, according to many Eastern spiritual disciplines, through which all universal energy merges with our own force field. It is also the contact center for the body and soul. When we feel centered, this point is in balance with all the other spiraling force fields of the chakras.

1. To get yourself centered, when you're lying in bed place your hands, with fingers touching, two inches below your navel. Just let them hover above your skin and feel the change of energy radiating from this spot.

2. Breathe slowly and deeply. Focus and meditate on this center of yourself for about three minutes.

If you practice this regularly for a few minutes before you go to bed and on waking, you will soon find you are centered and more able to engage in life, work with crystals successfully, and enhance your life in every way.

4. THE HEART CHAKRA

Situated behind the breastbone and in front of the spine, the heart chakra vibrates to the colors green and pink, and is the center of warm, loving feelings. This chakra is about true compassion, love, and spirituality. It directs our ability for self-love, as well as to give and to receive love. This is also the chakra connecting body and mind with spirit. When this chakra is low, you may be afraid of revealing your feelings for fear of getting hurt.

Wearing or carrying pink tourmaline or rose quartz will restore your compassion, empathy, and a sense of self-love. When this chakra is overactive you may be always helping everyone else and making sacrifices for loved ones, but never give any love to yourself. To subdue an overactive heart chakra, wear or carry malachite.

5. THE THROAT CHAKRA

The throat chakra is, of course, located in the lower end of the throat and is the center for thought, communication, music, speech, and writing. Vibrating to the color blue, when this chakra is out of balance you may feel timid, not say much, resent other people who say anything they like, misunderstand others, or just be unable to express your thoughts. Once balanced by wearing or carrying sapphire or aquamarine, you will be musically or artistically inspired, your communication skills will improve, and anything that you need to say will be said.

If you have an overactive throat chakra, you won't listen to anyone else and will think you know all the answers. You're verbose and angry with everyone around you. To correct and subdue an overactive throat chakra, wear or carry turquoise.

6. THE THIRD EYE

Located in the center of the brow, the third eye vibrates to the color indigo, or violet, and is concerned with inspiration, imagination, and psychic ability. When this chakra is not balanced you may be blind to the truth, non-assertive, afraid of success, and indecisive. You may not have any psychic sense, nor trust your intuition. To boost this chakra, the gemstone to wear or carry is the amethyst.

The third eye in balance can give you access to your higher self and altered states of consciousness. You feel "in tune" with the universal energy, and everything feels as if it's meant to be. You can see the truth of any matter and understand what people are really thinking or feeling. This will restore your intuitive and psychic nature, as well as give you strong imaginative and visualization powers. If this chakra is overactive, you can't come down to earth, you live with your head in the clouds and are totally irrational. Wearing lapis lazuli will subdue this chakra.

7. THE CROWN CHAKRA

Situated on the top of the head, this is the center for true spirituality and enlightenment. It allows for the inward flow of wisdom and brings the gift of cosmic consciousness. When this chakra is unbalanced there may be a constant sense of frustration, no spark of joy, and a frustrated sense of meaninglessness about everything. Balancing energy in this chakra gives you the ability to open up to the cosmic consciousness and connect to the light of the Universe flowing through all things. By wearing a diamond, you can boost the crown chakra and improve your own spiritual beliefs, open up a pathway and connection to other realms, or just aid your own spiritual development.

If this chakra is too active, you may think you're a guru, live in a spiritual haze, constantly talk to friends about your psychic powers, or you may be an idealist and eternal optimist who can't see the wood for the trees. To subdue this chakra, wear or carry opal.

CRYSTALS FOR PSYCHOLOGICAL AND EMOTIONAL HEALING

We can balance our chakras to restore some kind of order in our lives, but there are times when particular emotional wounds or psychological issues seem to seep up from the dark basement of our inner selves and darken the light of our personality.

For example, we may develop strong feelings of jealousy towards our partner, or envy towards a colleague. These feelings are often rooted in a deep fear of being abandoned, or low self-esteem. This is where crystals can be superb healing aids, either to boost a quality that we may be lacking, or to subdue an excess of an emotion that stops us being true to ourselves.

We haven't yet worked with many of the crystals on the following pages, and, of course, you may not want to invest in their magical powers yet. But all these stones will bring you a new perspective on healing and enhancement of your personal needs and desires.

Our moods, feelings, and hang-ups change as we evolve, so even if you can't relate to the emotional needs, spiritual longings, or life-enhancing suggestions over the following pages right now, you can dip into this part of the book as your needs change. But do try at least three exercises from each section, as working with some new crystals will enhance your awareness of how they enable us all to live a better lifestyle.

CRYSTAL	KEYWORDS
RHODOCROSITE	Self-acceptance, self-esteem
 PYRITE	Truth, courage
SMOKY QUARTZ	Self-belief, vitality
BLUE CHALCEDONY	Optimism, calm
 ROSE QUARTZ	Self-love, desire
JASPER	Confidence, honesty
KUNZITE	Renewal, transformation
CHRYSOCOLLA	Self-awareness, forgiveness

RHODOCROSITE

🗝 Self-awareness, truth,
and self-worth

With its lovely pink or orange bands,
rhodocrosite is the crystal most favored
to enhance self-awareness, compassion,
and unconditional love. The stone
promotes a sense of acceptance and
opens your mind to the truth of who you
are, allowing you to accept things you
may have denied. Rhodocrosite is both
comforting and positive. When worn or
carried on a daily basis, repressed
emotions such as anger or fear can be
acknowledged and released and
personal growth can take place. By
meditating with rhodocrosite you can
become more truthful about who you are
and your place in the world. The stone
also lifts depression and enhances a
positive outlook. It is also said to soothe
emotional stress, to overcome shyness
and nervousness, and to encourage
feelings of self-worth. If you feel unloved
or not worthy of love, meditating and
holding rhodocrosite will give you a
sense of your true value as a loveable
human being who has a right to have
that love just by being on this earth.

ENHANCING SELF-AWARENESS

Hold your rhodocrosite stone for five
minutes while you calm your mind and
relax, or do your meditation. Once you
have centered and stilled yourself, ask the
stone to help you to accept who you are,
bring to light your true nature, or to give
out love and be loved without conditions.

Afterward, repeat the following affirmation:

*"I will be free from emotional pain,
and will be aware of the light
within myself as it flows
through all things, the light of the
Universe itself."*

PYRITE
⚬━ Motivation

Also known as fool's gold because of its beautiful golden light, this stone was used by the Aztecs to make highly polished mirrors, which were used for seeing into the future. The color gold has always been a symbol of success, power, the sun, royalty, light, and adventure. Working with pyrite restores one's sense of power and perseverance when the going gets tough. It is a fabulous crystal to relieve sadness, melancholy, or just the angst of being human. Instead of seeing life filled with doom and gloom, pyrite stirs you to change your perception, to see the positive, the glass half full rather than half empty. Molehills no longer become mountains—they get trampled on. Pyrite urges you to search for solutions to troubling thoughts or feelings, or those you've been dwelling on for some time. In this way, pyrite helps you to see what truly lies behind other people's words and actions, and reveals the truth that we have just the same weaknesses as others. Pyrite empowers you with courage and releases inhibitions, allowing you to act rather than hesitate, to be who you are, rather than fear who you are.

SELF-EMPOWERMENT

Once your mind is stilled, and you're calm, gaze at one face of your pyrite stone and imagine it is like a polished mirror, about to reveal the future. Imagine what you want most in the world, something so desirable that it makes you smile. Gaze deeper into the stone. Can you see yourself smiling? Now say to the stone:

"My beautiful desire will be mine one day, now I lift my spirit to the golden light that you carry for me, as I carry you."

Carry this stone with you as often as you can.

SMOKY QUARTZ
Dealing with negative thinking

This mesmerizing crystal was once used as a mystical power stone in many cultures. To the Druids, it was the stone of earth gods and goddesses. Grounding and protective, smoky quartz is renowned for clearing your mind of negativity, depression, and resentment. It evokes a feeling of well-being and a realization that you can let go of those beliefs or expectations which are no longer of any value to your personal growth. Relieving stress and anger, it gives you the belief to follow your convictions, and to resolve problems and take responsibility for your choices. Smoky quartz also grounds you, allowing you to see that by being part of the world, rather than hiding from it, you can create your own reality and manifest your dreams. By wearing smoky quartz, you will be able to concentrate and communicate successfully and let go of old patterns of behavior that have created tension or stress in your life. If you hold two pieces of the stone in each hand for a few minutes, angling the points away from your body, you will banish sadness, stress, and negativity. Then point them back toward you for a few minutes to invite positive energy back.

DISSOLVING NEGATIVITY

Place a ring of five smoky quartz crystals on a table with their points facing inward. Sit quietly before the table as you write your name on a piece of paper and place it in the middle of the circle. Now say aloud:

"These five stones will dissolve my negativity, enhance my vitality, and let my life flow with joy."

Take the stones and carry them with you to thoroughly energize you with positive vibrations.

BLUE CHALCEDONY

⊶ Stop worrying

The "Speaker's Stone," as it was once known, was said to have been worn as a pendant by the great Roman orator Cicero. This delicate blue stone enhances all speaking skills, such as learning new languages, wit and humor, and even promotes telepathic power. Because of its influence on the mind, it channels away flurries of worry and anxiety that can overcome even the most carefree of us. The stone will help to rid you of all self-doubt, replacing it with a lighthearted optimism and *joie de vivre*. Blue chalcedony allows you to accept change and helps you to live life for the moment, rather than worrying or imagining a doom-laden future. Its timeless quality gives a sense of timelessness to life, too. So instead of picking over past hurts, or fearing the day ahead, you can get on with the present and live in the now. If you are prone to irrational anger, fear, or even panic attacks, the stone helps to absorb the tricks of the mind, replacing them with a sense of calm and the ability to rationalize.

A SENSE OF CALM

Hold a piece of the stone in your hands, and with your eyes closed, clear your mind of all thoughts as in the meditation technique on pages 136–137. Now imagine you are sailing on a ship in the middle of a calm ocean. There is nothing to see for miles and miles, just the endless horizon and blue sky, blue water. It is peaceful, tranquil, you have nothing to worry about except—will you ever see land again? Will the ship get you to your destination? Hold the stone tighter and feels its power flowing through you, removing all worry and fear of getting to the shore, because the stone knows that even though you can't see it, the shore is there. Come out of your imagination and see the stone in your hands, reminding you that the shore is there because the shore is you.

ROSE QUARTZ
Love and compassion

Sometimes known as the Love or Heart Stone, rose quartz has been used in jewelry and as a talisman of love for over six thousand years. With its delicate rose pink veins, it is worn today to attract love. If placed in the southwest corner of your home it will invoke love and compassion in your life. It can also be used to attract romance and promote sexual intimacy, or can be placed in the east corner of your home to develop a closer bond with family or friends. This is a stone of sensuality. It loves you and embraces you with its gift of love, awakening you to the real joys and longings of your heart and soul. As a stone of romantic love, rose quartz is a powerful aphrodisiac, stimulating your desires. Wear or carry it to heal any emotional or love wounds. If you have loved and lost, and fear you will never love again, place it by your bed to receive its loving energy. Rose quartz gently brings nurture, comfort, and inner nourishment to a stone cold heart. It can be used in spells to change an aloof stranger to an intimate lover. If you have never experienced real love, then rose quartz helps you to develop a positive self-image that attracts others to you.

LOVING THE BEAUTY WITHIN YOU

First of all hug yourself. Wrap your arms around yourself and really hug yourself, as if you were meeting an old friend that you loved. Keep doing this for about a minute until you feel warm and loved, embraced and appreciated. Focus on how good you feel to be hugged, and how much better you feel afterward. Now take your rose quartz crystal and tenderly hold it in your hands, showing it that you care and it will be loved and hugged too. Place it by your bed to attract love in your life and to promote your own ability to see beauty in others and most of all in yourself.

JASPER

○━ To clear guilt and blame

In medieval Europe, it was believed that wearing jasper engraved with an image of a hare protected the wearer from attack by demons, and if engraved with a dog, it protected against venom or dog attacks. A sacred magical protection stone, it was also known as "the Rain Bringer," and was used to conjure up the rain and save harvests in periods of drought, or to calm storms at sea and ensure safe passage to ships and sailors. This is an excellent stone for boosting confidence, but most importantly for standing up for what you believe in without feeling guilty for believing it. Jasper strengthens your emotional nature and eases stress. It invites honesty and helps you recognize and get rid of feelings of guilt or blame. It inspires you to move forward assertively and to not be manipulated by the need for external approval, one of the root causes of guilt.

BANISHING GUILT

Think about something you feel guilty about. For example, you neglected to tell your partner you'd be late home from work because you'd be stopping off for a drink with a work colleague. You immediately feel guilt-ridden because you know they wouldn't approve. This common type of guilt is based on the need for approval.

Take a piece of jasper in your writing hand, face a mirror, and reveal your guilty experience out loud to yourself. For example, "It gave me great pleasure to have a drink with my friend, and if my partner doesn't approve, then it is their opinion, not mine."

Repeat your "guilt trip" three times as you tighten your grip on the jasper. Then, finally, say out loud three times:

> "I no longer feel guilty for..... I simply don't share their opinion."

Approval is an opinion, and an opinion is a value judgment. Jasper dissolves your sense of guilt generated by other people's approval or disapproval and makes you love yourself enough not to be beholden to those opinions.

KUNZITE

○━━ Loss, separation, and heartbreak

The beauty of lilac, pink, and clear kunzite lies not just in its delicate coloring, but in its ability to enhance universal love when worn or carried. It is this sense of being loved, from within as well as without, that helps you through emotional disharmony or the negative feelings of loss and separation. Kunzite dispels this negativity and enables you to overcome heartbreak after any kind of relationship split. It also promotes inspiration and intuition, and a sense that you can let go of the past. With its high vibrational energy it generates a positive sense of the here and now, rather than letting sad thoughts stop you from moving on. Kunzite encourages tolerance for oneself, as well as compassion for others. Its potent energy cuts through disillusion or fear of what is to come, and activates your desire to start again and to express your feelings openly, which in turn means that you can slowly become free from the chains of debilitating emotions.

FREEDOM FROM EMOTIONAL CHAINS

Wear kunzite, preferably as a pendant (it works best when activating the heart chakra), for the day and observe your own reactions to people you know or strangers you first meet. Notice when they come into your personal space whether you either accept them straight away or hold something back of yourself. Then when they leave, notice how you accept their leaving or are glad for them to be gone. Kunzite will help you to see how those that you accept will always stay in your heart, wherever they are, and that they have never really truly gone, nor are they lost. They are somewhere, whether in this tangible world, or in another realm.

CHRYSOCOLLA

○━► For truth and clarity

This lovely blue-green stone gives clarity of mind and enables you to see the truth of any matter. If you need to express your feelings or need to know what you truly feel about someone, wearing chrysocolla will promote deeper wisdom and self-awareness. This serene turquoise stone calms and dissolves negative energy, brings positive thoughts, and strengthens self-belief. Energizing the power of words in your life, the stone helps you to teach others what you know, and also to show that you are fearless about your own opinions or values. Clarity brings understanding and forgiveness, and it is this forgiveness, for both yourself and for others, which is at the heart of compassion. On an emotional level, chrysocolla enables you to know the difference between tactless expression and the virtue of keeping silent. Silence often speaks volumes, while speaking up can reveal nothing. This stone's soothing energy dispels highly charged emotional situations or angry words and allows your truth to be shared.

TO PROMOTE SELF-BELIEF

Light a white candle, relax, meditate for a few minutes with the stone in your hands, and then place chrysocolla on the table in front of you. Gaze into the depths of the stone and imagine what truth you would like to know. For example:

> • Who can I trust at work?
>
> • What direction should I take in my career?

Imagine there in the depths of the stone you are in perfect harmony with the workings of the Universe and you are being told the truthful answer to your question. Imagine that this silence speaks more than a thousand words, and as you continue to gaze into the stone, you "hear" the answer.

CRYSTALS FOR SPIRITUAL DEVELOPMENT

Our spiritual nature is just as important as our psychological one. Whether you believe in an afterlife or not, if you're reading this book then it's likely that you at least have some kind of belief about your spiritual nature, your soul, and the purpose for your existence.

Healing ourselves of psychological debris is one thing, but trying to heal or balance a side of ourselves that is by its very mystical nature unknown is more challenging—yet ultimately satisfying. It is about giving ourselves up to the mystery of this inner place and attempting in some way to get closer to the universal energy from which we came and to which we will return. Being part of the "soul" of the cosmos, we can at least try to reconnect to it, or show that our minds and emotions can be in harmony with that universal soul.

The stones in this section will help you to meditate, evolve, and develop your higher states of consciousness so that you can tune in to the cosmic vibrations and feel at peace or at one with the universe. I have chosen stones that help with meditational states, getting in touch with your "higher self" or "inner guide," as well as stones for deeper spiritual exploration and helping to develop your psychic powers.

CRYSTAL	KEYWORDS
KYANITE	Meditation, spiritual integrity
MOONSTONE	Intuition, inner vision
BLUE SELENITE	Sixth sense, psychic power
FLUORITE	Psychic protection
OPAL	Spiritual cleansing
NUMMITE	Clairvoyance, spiritual contact
TANZANITE	Supernatural power

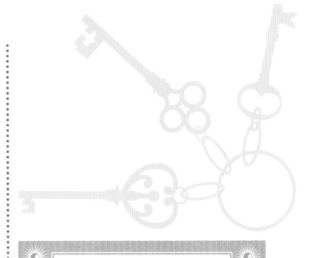

KYANITE

⚷ **Getting in touch with your higher self**

One of the best known stones for opening up the mind centers and reaching into the depths of our higher or spiritual selves, kyanite is excellent for meditation. This extraordinary crystal also enhances telepathic and psychic abilities, and provides a link for transmitting or receiving healing energy. It immediately aligns the chakras, bringing tranquility and a calming effect to the whole being. It is an exceptional stone for achieving deep meditative states. Kyanite, like citrine, doesn't accumulate or retain negative energy, and therefore never needs cleaning. When you wear or carry this stone, any sense of external fate becomes mere illusion, and you begin to realize that you create your own destiny. If you believe in reincarnation and the law of karma, then in this life at least you will now know how to balance any disharmonies of your past lives. Most importantly, kyanite promotes spiritual maturity and integrity, and allows you to get in touch with that higher or spiritual self.

SPIRITUAL AWAKENING

Place eight small kyanite stones pointing to the eight compass points, north, northwest, west, southwest, south, southeast, east, northeast, radiating out from a central ninth piece of kyanite.

Over a series of eight sessions, relax and go into a meditational state, and focus on one of the blades only, changing to another the next night, and so on. As you gaze at the blade, imagine you are walking along it to find your spiritual self. Let yourself be guided by the blades as you say, "I will listen to the inner voice of myself as I walk my pathway, knowing that I am in touch with the universal light." Once you have "walked" all eight paths, you will be more aware of that inner voice and its ability to guide you.

MOONSTONE
⊶ Enhancing intuition

Moonstones have always been thought to be linked to the power of the lunar cycle, which itself attunes to the rhythms of the oceans. The Romans believed the stone held an image of the moon goddess Diana, and that wearing the stone bestowed the owner with love, wisdom, prophecy, and second sight. This lovely translucent crystal was also an amulet of protection for travelers and a gift between lovers to enhance passion. The moon itself is a potent symbol of all things feminine, the rhythms of nature, the sensitive, nurturing powers of all aspects of life. Moonstones bring inspiration, flashes of insight, and stop you giving up on your intuition, instead promoting it so that you see from your third eye or sixth sense, rather than react from only your common sense. Wearing this stone promotes clarity of the mind and inner vision, and keeps you focused while in a meditative state of awareness. White moonstone carries the energy of the new moon at the height of its power, stimulating psychic perception, vision, and dream work.

INTUITION ENHANCEMENT

When it's dark, find somewhere quiet and comfortable to sit—all the better if you can do this under the light of the full moon. If not, light a cream-colored candle. Hold the moonstone between your hands and as you gaze at it in the muted light, imagine yourself entering the depths of the stone. Here you meet your intuitive self, and as you merge with your intuitive self you feel as if you are journeying among the stars. Now say:

> *"I welcome my intuitive self and the joy of being at one with the Universe."*

Gently come out of your visualization and place the stone under your pillow for one lunar cycle to help you listen to your intuitive voice and guide.

BLUE SELENITE

⊶ **Psychic power and clairvoyance**

We've already come across white selenite among the astrological stones in Chapter One, but blue selenite is especially effective for enhancing your own psychic powers via its influence on the third eye chakra. Selenite can also be used when meditating to ensure clarity in your spiritual understanding of the Universe and your place in it. Clairvoyance, from the French for "seeing clearly," is the ability to be aware of other people, or of those who have passed into the spirit world. Clear awareness, referred to as "siddhis" in Hindu texts, is a kind of perfect state of awareness achieved through meditation. There are other forms of "sixth sensing," such as clairaudience (clear listening) and clairsentience (picking up the vibrational energy of people). Selenite can enhance these natural abilities if you are keen to become more in tune with any of those psychic senses.

SIXTH SENSE STARTER

We all have flashes of insight, when our sixth sense comes to work suddenly and we can "see" the answer to a problem, or we "know" X is going to phone us just as we are about to pick up the phone to call them. To enhance this skill, carry or wear selenite for the day. Each time you are about to turn a corner in the street, or think about someone you haven't seen for a long time, hold the selenite in your hand and imagine the person coming to you, calling you up, or just imagine something you'd like to happen that day and see it manifest.

FLUORITE
Spiritual protection
Available in a range of colors, including clear, purple, brown, green, blue, and rainbow, fluorite is one of the favored psychic protection stones. It not only keeps negative energy away from you, but helps you to understand when external influences could be harmful, including psychic manipulation from others. It is also highly effective as protection against geopathic stress and other electromagnetic negativity. Keep a stone beside your computer to dispel negative energy. With its power to connect you to the Universe, it aids with meditation and a feeling of safety. Enhancing purity of the chakras and awareness of the Hara, it gently cleanses and restores balance and order while dissolving illusions in the tangible reality that you see before you.

SPIRITUAL PROTECTION

Light a white candle, then place three pieces of fluorite on the table in front of you. Take one in each hand and leave the third on the table. Feel the weight of the two in your hands—are they the same or is there a difference, even the minutest difference in weight? Can you sense this? As you weigh and measure in your mind you will begin to notice that there is no difference between you and the stone. As you meditate on the weights of the stones, you are both the two stones, equal and weightless, protected by their power. As you gaze at the third stone, this becomes your "scrying" stone, always there to protect you so you can see what is coming and act accordingly. Come out of your meditation gently, then keep all three stones to help connect you to your own power and protect you from negative energy.

OPAL

○━┐ Spiritual strength

Once thought by the ancients to be the stone that embodied all the other gemstones because of its iridescent colors, it was worn to improve sight, heal eye problems, and bestow good luck on the wearer. Opal is used by shamans to invoke cosmic visions and for crossing over to the spiritual world. It is also known to cleanse the spiritual and emotional self and brings optimism and joy to everything we do. Use opal to release inhibitions and enhance your awareness of your connection to the cosmos. The stone promotes the ability to work with your intuition and insight. Carry or wear it as a protective stone while doing any spiritual work. Opal absorbs your feelings and thoughts and reflects them back, enhancing your self-worth and sense of spirit and soul.

PSYCHIC STRENGTH

To invoke protection and strength, program an opal to work for you with its vibrational link to the spirit world. Place four candles on the table at the points of the compass, north, south, east, and west. Then place an opal in the center. Light the candles, relax, and focus on the opal. Welcome the spirits of the four directions, by saying, "Welcome spirit of the north, with this opal, and empower me with your protection and strength." Say this to each of the directions and then take your opal in your hands and welcome it as your personal strength talisman.

NUMMITE

o—⟶ **Magic and spiritual exploration**

Often known as the Sorcerer's Stone, nummite is the perfect choice if you are thinking of working with magic or spells. Worn as a talisman, it not only increases your own personal charisma, but enhances your clairvoyant or intuitive powers. Place a piece of nummite beside you when working with other divination tools, such as the tarot, runes, or astrological charts, to boost your ability to read the symbols and signs around you. The stone also deepens your connection to the natural world and the cosmos, relieving fear of the unknown and strengthening your contact with the spiritual realm. Offering spiritual protection, it enhances all forms of magical exploration, occult study, or simply a feeling that you can create your own destiny and manifest your deepest desires.

NUMMITE SPELL

Cast a spell with nummite to enhance your own sense of magic and charisma. Place a piece on a table between two white lit candles, with a mirror propped up behind so that you can see your reflection. Gaze at the reflection of the nummite stone for a while as you relax into a state of calmness. Keep gazing at the stone in the mirror, but notice the candle flames, too, as well as your own face in the distance. Repeat the following spell three times to invoke the power of the crystal into your world:

"This stone is from the past, and
speaks the future too;
Its present is a gift to bring me
magic fine and true."

TANZANITE

Psychic power

Tanzanite is an excellent crystal for exploration of your psychic powers. It helps to take you gently into the unknown magic of yourself, and can be used as a talisman or carried to enhance all aspects of supernatural power. Its vibrational energy is highly protective and invokes a safe energy when connecting to higher realms. It also helps you to enter a deeper meditational state. Illuminating the mind, it stirs you to understand that beyond the mind is another aspect of yourself: your soul. When working with cleansing or awakening your chakras, you can use tanzanite to open the third eye chakra. Hold the stone to the center of your forehead and turn it clockwise very slowly. Then, when you want to close down this center, turn it counterclockwise.

PSYCHIC ALIGNMENT

During a full moon, place tanzanite on your window ledge and leave it overnight to charge it with lunar energy. The next day, carry it everywhere with you. Notice how it lightens your mind, removes negative thoughts, and allows you to both understand and release intuitive flashes or experience amazing insights. It will make you realize that you can develop any psychic skill you want to, such as working with angels, the tarot, or simply working with crystals, as you are doing right now.

SPIRITUAL PURPOSE

When you feel that you have no spiritual sense, or that you've lost all contact with your psychic abilities, do this exercise to restore and reinforce all available energy that will put you back on track with your own psychic powers.

Take a piece of each of the following you have so far used in this section:

KYANITE
KEY QUALITIES: meditation, spiritual integrity

MOONSTONE
KEY QUALITIES: intuition, inner vision

BLUE SELENITE
KEY QUALITIES: sixth sense, psychic power

FLUORITE
KEY QUALITIES: psychic protection

OPAL
KEY QUALITIES: spiritual cleansing

NUMMITE
KEY QUALITIES: clairvoyance, spiritual contact

TANZANITE
KEY QUALITIES: supernatural power

1. Place the stones in a circle in the order given, starting with kyanite to the north of the circle and moving round from east to west. In the middle of the circle place a lit candle. Write the following letters on a piece of paper and place it beneath the circle (these are the magic letter of the stones):

KYMYESFLOPANUTAN

2. Close your eyes and gaze at the letters while you say the spell below to enhance your own spiritual power.

> Oh stones of power, bring me the joy
> Of love and healing, high and true
> Of breath and sky, of that which falls
> Of wonders known, or those so few
> We are of One, and One is all
> With this I'm blessed with crystals true.

3. Now blow out your candle. Fold the paper and place in a safe place for one lunar cycle, then throw it away, but keep your stones safe forever.

STONES FOR LIFE ENHANCEMENT

When you want to improve or enhance your general lifestyle, there are many stones you can choose from, and many you will discover that you love or prefer to work with as you continue on your crystal journey.

The ones I have selected here are perfect for all kinds of personal empowerment, self-love, passion, and integrity. After all, where would we be without a sense of self-reliance and responsibility, inspiration, fortune, or meaning in life? Once our psychological and spiritual selves are in harmony, and we can truly accept who we are as individuals, we can then begin to enhance our lives in a positive and dynamic way.

As we come to the end of the book, these final eight stones make invaluable additions to your collection. With the main stones that we've worked with so far, you've gradually developed an awareness that every crystal has its own personal magic. Yet what you will find as you continue working with crystals is that there is one stone out of all of these, or perhaps from those you might not have yet come across, that is your stone; in other words, it is a reflection of you. I think I would call this your "soul-mate stone" which, very soon, you will discover for yourself when you're browsing New Age stores, or just by picking one up by chance. Or maybe you have already. I think by now you have realized that these crystals are your lifelong friends, so honor their magical influence in your life.

CRYSTAL	KEYWORDS
APATITE	Confidence, creativity
CHAROITE	Living in the moment
FIRE AGATE	Self-belief, integrity
IOLITE	Responsibility, clarity
AZURITE	Inspiration, innovation
SUNSTONE	Opportunity, prosperity
SARDONYX	Exploration, stability
GREEN AVENTURINE	Good fortune, motivation

APATITE

○━╼ Personal empowerment

Apatite comes in a number of colors; yellow is the rarest, but blue is available everywhere. This inspirational stone enhances personal power to achieve your goals. As a stone of motivation, apatite banishes apathy, promoting instead a thirst for knowledge and truth. This is a stone that makes things happen, or makes things manifest in the world. If you can get hold of the yellow variety, you will be blessed with healthy assertiveness, a passion for life, and a sense of self-confidence. All apatite enhances creativity, and this stone of vision and extrovert energy is the best friend you can take with you to enhance your communication powers during any business dealings or other negotiations.

ACHIEVEMENT OF GOALS

Place a piece of apatite in your pocket or wear it as a pendant for a day. Throughout the day observe how, when you want something to happen, it happens. For example, you want a deal finalized or someone to send you a kind message, and it does. Place the stone beside your bed that night, and the next day you will feel a real passion for life and awareness of a new set of goals.

CHAROITE
⚷ Self-love

This beautiful purple stone's name is derived from the Chara River in eastern Siberia, the only place in the world where it is found. This crystal makes you more aware of the present moment, and that whatever you are doing right now is right for that moment, and thus helps to make you love being yourself in that moment. As a stone of self-acceptance, when worn or carried, it enhances your self-worth, bringing you closer to understanding why you attract others to you and how loving yourself will mean others will love you better. Its cleansing energy aligns mind, soul, and spirit and promotes a sense of unconditional love towards others, too. Charoite inspires a sense of letting go of negativity, and of moving on to be truly at one with yourself.

BEING AT ONE

Cup the palms of your hands around your stone, without covering it totally. Once you are calm and serene, and in a meditational state, gaze down into your magical purple pool of charoite and just concentrate on the color in the moment. Repeat in your head or out loud:

"This is Now, this moment is Now, there is no other past or future moment, I am in the eternal Now."

Repeat this as many times as you like, until you feel totally at one with the moment. Come out of your meditation and thank the stone for letting you see yourself as eternal. Take it wherever you go to instill self-love and self-worth and to attract others to you.

FIRE AGATE

o—x Passion and integrity

Medieval alchemists used fire agate in experiments to turn lead into gold, because it was believed to contain the essence of fire, one of the elements needed to achieve perfect gold, whether real gold or the gold of the soul. This crystal of utter self-belief and integrity promotes high standards of behavior, both in yourself and others, as well as enhancing passion in life and love. Wearing or carrying this stone enables you to take decisive action when the circumstances are not clear or are confused by others. It enhances a true reconnection to one's deepest desires, giving the gift of courage and risk-taking. Fire agate also promotes self-acceptance and confidence, encouraging you to speak the truth and show that you are utterly faithful to your own goals.

SPEAKING THE TRUTH

Place three red candles in the shape of a pyramid on the table before you. Place a piece of fire agate in the middle of the triangle and light the candles. Sit for a while as the flames flicker and see if you can see the essence of fire within the stone. As you start to glimpse this luminous quality, also begin to feel it reflected in yourself. Feel the warmth of the fire flow through you, bringing you passion, confidence, ambition, and self-determination. Blow out the candles, then hold the fire agate in your hand and feel its energy burning into you, as you realize you have aligned to this powerful alchemical energy of transforming yourself from lead to gold.

IOLITE

⊶ Responsibility and order

Often referred to as water sapphire, iolite, when looked at from different angles, appears to change color from violet-blue to yellow, gray, and even a clear light blue. Iolite strengthens your desire to take on responsibility and see projects through to a conclusion. It enhances self-assurance and endurance in times of difficulty. This stone restores a sense of perspective if you feel confused, chaotic or lost, and inspires you to bring order to your life through practical means. Carry or wear iolite if family members have high expectations of you, or if your career path was chosen for you because of clan connections. Iolite enables you to identify whether your expectations are your own or other people's, and to see how you can take responsibility for your own choices and order your life accordingly.

RESPONSIBILITY TEST

Take two pieces of iolite and place them on two different pieces of paper. On one of the papers write, "Am I living by my expectations?" On the other, write, "Am I living by other people's expectations?" On both write underneath, "My responsibility is to…"

Hold the two stones and thank them for their help before placing them on the papers, and then leave them in place overnight. Before you go to bed, ask the stones to bring you the answer to the questions, either via your dreams, a sign, or an unexpected way, but you will know when you experience the solution the next day. The next evening, take up the stones, throw away one of the papers, and on the remaining paper, fill in the last word(s) after "My responsibility is to…" For example, you may write that your responsibility is to "myself," or "my children," or "aged parents," or "my spiritual journey." Whatever the truth that has been revealed, now you can start to take responsibility for your life.

AZURITE

 Inspiration

Named after its deep azure blue color, azurite is a naturally "soft" stone. The ancient Taoists called it the Stone of Heaven, believing it would open the gateways to the starry heavens above. Revered by Greeks and Romans for its visionary insights and healing powers, azurite inspires, yet tempers the mind. While it alleviates worry, indecision, or confusion, it also invokes flashes of inspiration and new perceptions. Azurite stimulates all of your mind, encouraging the study of new or challenging subjects. It enhances focus and concentration, memory and innovative thinking, and is of great benefit if you need inspiration for creative work.

POSITIVE DIRECTION

Azurite is best worn or carried. It is known as a "rubbing stone" (because it likes to be touched to release its energy), so it needs to be held and gently rubbed with your fingers on a daily basis. Troublesome thoughts will disappear and inspirational ones take their place. When you get up in the morning, take the stone in your hand and ask it for inspiration throughout the day. Every time you have to make a decision, rub the stone and you will immediately know which is the right path to follow.

SUNSTONE

⚬—⚹ Abundance

This yellow, orange, or sometimes reddish iridescent stone was once thought to represent the Hindu sun god, Surya. With its joyful colors and lovely reflective quality, sunstone brings abundance to anyone who works with it as a true friend. Sunstone was used in medieval times to decorate goblets and plates, and was believed to counteract poison and induce kingly strength. Known as the stone of abundance, sunstone inspires you to nurture yourself, to enjoy life to the full, and enhances a sense of your own independence and originality. Traditionally, the stone is linked to good luck and fortune, so it can help show you your real talents, also attracting fame and prosperity. In the workplace, sunstone brings opportunities for leadership or promotion. Worn as a pendant, sunstone brings the wisdom of the soul into balance with the mind's inspiration.

GOOD LUCK MEDITATION

Enter into your meditational or relaxed state. Hold your sunstone in your hands and imagine you are the sun god or goddess as you travel across the skies by day in your golden chariot, burning a beautiful trail of sparkling golden light behind you. As you look behind, all the twinkling lights turn to sunstones and fall to earth. Below you are thousands and millions of people; some know the value of sunstone, but most merely kick the stones away, or dig them into the earth. But there is one who picks up a stone and places it on their window ledge to capture you, the Sun, every morning in its reflective light. You acknowledge the person, knowing your stone is safe with them, because that person is you.

SARDONYX

Meaning in life

This stone is formed from two stones, onyx and carnelian, and embodies these two energies working together to create a stabilizing yet "brave heart" stone. If you have been searching for meaning in your life, wearing or working with this stone may help you to find the answer to it. Sardonyx has a positive vibration and helps you to attract new friendships and bring stability to all kinds of partnership. A stone of integrity and willpower, it helps you to make decisions, see the truth behind others' exterior motives, and to know deep down inside what is right for your future. Grounding yet stimulating, sardonyx motivates you to find a quest in life, and to know why you are here. It is the stone for exploring and crossing philosophical boundaries where you can stay down to earth while searching for a meaningful existence.

MISSION AND QUEST

Sit cross-legged somewhere quiet and calm your mind. (If you're unable to sit cross-legged, draw a spiral on a piece of paper and imagine yourself starting at the outside and walking inward.) Place two pieces of sardonyx beside your feet and now imagine yourself walking between them in a figure of eight (or along the spiral). As you walk the path of infinity, repeat the following:

"Stone of Meaning, send me the answer to all that is and all that I am. As I am part of the cosmic Oneness, let me realize what I already know."

Gather your stones and wear or carry them for three days, and you will be motivated to find your own quest in life.

GREEN AVENTURINE
⚬⇁ Opportunities

Known as the stone of opportunity, green aventurine attracts good fortune to you, but also makes sure you're in the right place at the right time. This curious ability to enhance synchronicity in your life allows you to break free of old habits, regrets, and negativity and see where opportunity is to be found. With green aventurine, chance and opportunity are inevitable, and along with those chances comes a confidence and a belief that you can take advantage of the right moment. The stone also enhances your creativity and motivation, reinforces decisiveness, and yet invokes a great sense of fun and openness to the ideas of others and the unknown. Thought to be the luckiest of all crystals, it can even manifest prosperity and wealth, and is a handy talisman in any competition or game of chance.

OPPORTUNITY KNOCKS

Take a piece of green aventurine in your hands and relax and float downstream in the boat of your mind for a few minutes. Let the boat take you down to the sea where it comes to a gentle rest on the stony seashore.

Imagine you climb out of the boat ready for adventure, for some great opportunity to come your way. Will you seize the moment? Will you take a chance? Will you know it when it comes? Hold the green aventurine tightly in your hands and then gaze into its depths.

There on the seashore is a stranger who beckons you, a kind face, a golden light emanating from their aura, and they too hold a piece of green aventurine in their hands. This is the time to act, it is meant to be, the synchronicity of the moment is great, you are ready now to move on and take a leap into the world of magical living. You take the stranger's hand, knowing it is time to take a leap of faith and a breath of adventure.

CONCLUSION

"The tree which moves some to tears of joy is in the eyes of others only a green thing that stands in the way. Some see nature all ridicule and deformity... and some scarce see nature at all. But to the eyes of the man of imagination, nature is imagination itself." WILLIAM BLAKE

William Blake understood magic and imagination and how they are one and the same. If you want to make something happen, you only have to imagine it, believe in it, and ask your crystals to help you connect to your own magical power. William Blake also understood nature and the substance of nature. He saw "a World in a Grain of Sand and a Heaven in a Wild Flower." What you are seeing in these ancient stones is both heaven and the world, and also that "all is one and one is all."

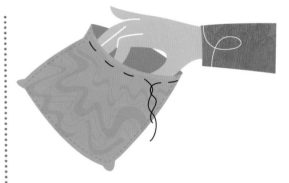

By now, you will have worked with many of the crystals in this book. Some you may have found fascinating, others meaningless—it all depends on your personal needs and how you perceive the world at any one moment in time. The crystals we choose to work with at any time in our life truly mirror our outer state. So, for example, if you love gazing at the green aventurine sitting on your desk, then it's more than likely you would love some fame and fortune right now. If you can't resist touching and holding your beautifully polished obsidian pendant, then you are probably fearful of the world and need some psychic protection for the time being. Our moods, feelings, and thoughts change as we make our journey through life, and so does our choice of crystals.

Although our character doesn't change innately, we do discover hidden potential in ourselves which may have been unconsciously suppressed or denied. For example, you've lived under the expectations of your family, peers, or society, and suddenly discover that you have a totally different viewpoint than you were "supposed" to have. You rebel, you move away, friends say, "You've changed," when in fact you're just becoming who you really are.

So, if you look with care, and ask the Universe to help you too, you will also discover the richness and beauty within yourself, whether you want to call that an individual soul or a universal one. You may have already found a true crystal friend that you can't be without right now, although that choice of crystal friend may change once you no longer have any need for its help.

Whatever you have experienced by working with crystals in this book, I hope it gives you not only a thirst for more knowledge, but more practice for loving your crystal friends as they come and go in your life. It is these friends who will show you the way, a bit like the day on the beach when I "saw" the Universe, not in a grain of sand, but in a simple black stone of truth.

All stones carry this truth, as do all grains of sand. It is this interconnection to all things, including your own magical power, that crystals will help you to discover—the experience of "one is all."

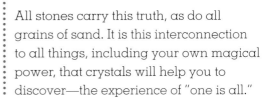

CRYSTALS GLOSSARY

RED CARNELIAN

GARNET

BLOODSTONE

RUBY

RED TIGER'S EYE

RED JASPER

RED AGATE

FIRE AGATE

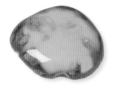

AMBER

TIGER'S EYE

ORANGE CARNELIAN

SARDONYX

ORANGE/
YELLOW CALCITE

CITRINE

APATITE

CHRYSOBERYL

SUNSTONE

YELLOW FLUORITE

YELLOW TOPAZ

FLUORITE

EMERALD

PERIDOT

MALACHITE

AMAZONITE

GREEN AVENTURINE

JADE

GREEN TOURMALINE

TURQUOISE

CHRYSOCOLLA

AQUAMARINE

LABRADORITE

BLUE TOPAZ

AZURITE

BLUE LACE AGATE

BLUE TOURMALINE

LAPIS LAZULI

TANZANITE

CHALCEDONY

KYANITE

BLUE SELENITE

SAPPHIRE

PURPLE SAPPHIRE

PURPLE FLUORITE

SUGILITE

AMETHYST

NATURAL AGATE

IOLITE

RHODOCHROSITE

CHAROITE

PINK TOURMALINE

ROSE QUARTZ

BRONZITE

MAHOGANY OBSIDIAN

ONYX

JET

NUMMITE

BLACK TOURMALINE

BLACK SAPPHIRE

OBSIDIAN

MAGNETITE

CLEAR/WHITE QUARTZ

MOONSTONE

PYRITE

DIAMOND

SILVER/WHITE TOPAZ

WHITE SELENITE

KUNZITE

OPAL

SMOKY QUARTZ

HEMATITE

GLOSSARY

ARCHETYPE
A universal energy or pattern of behavior which operates autonomously in the depths of the human psyche.

ASTROLOGY
An ancient system of divination which studies the patterns and placement of the planets of the solar system as they appear to travel through the zodiac belt.

BAGUA
The magical compass used in the ancient Chinese art of feng shui. It can be used to determine which areas of your home to place certain crystals for harmony and enhancement.

CHAKRA
A spinning vortex of invisible energy with seven or more "centers" throughout the body.

DEDICATION
A way to empower your crystal with positive energy to help you to fulfill your goals.

EARTH ACUPUNCTURE
The practice of burying crystals in the ground or laying them in a grid system in order to balance and create harmony in the environment.

ELECTROMAGNETIC ENERGY
Energy that is emitted or reflected by objects in the form of electrical and magnetic waves.

FENG SHUI
The ancient Chinese art of placement and balance in the home and/or environment to ensure good business, harmony, love, and success.

GEMSTONE
Also known as gem, jewel, semi-precious and precious stone, the gemstone is a piece of mineral which, in cut and polished form, is used to make jewelry or other adornments. The most well-known precious gemstones are diamonds, rubies, emeralds, and sapphires However, rare minerals such as lapis lazuli are also used for jewelry, and are often

considered to be gemstones too but are classified, like most other crystals, as semi-precious stones.

GEOMANCY

An ancient form of divination in which the marks and patterns of stones, earth, and sand on the ground were "read." In the Renaissance, it was popularized by occultists such as Cornelius Agrippa as a symbolic form of divination magic.

GEOPATHIC STRESS

A type of energy created by disturbances and negative power from underground water courses, power lines, and negative ley lines (earth energy). It runs through or above the ground and can pollute and influence people and buildings.

GRIDDING

The placing of crystals in specific patterns around a building, room, or person for enhancement or protection.

GROUNDING

A way of creating and balancing one's own personal energy to gain a firm sense of connectedness to the Earth.

MAGMA

From a Greek word meaning "thick" and "unguent," magma is a mixture of molten or semi-molten rock, gases, and solids that is found beneath the surface of the Earth.

ORACLE

A message sent by ancient Greek gods, such as Apollo, and transmitted through a high priestess at the god's temple. It was originally advice or a prediction about an individual's future The word is used today to describe portents or the energy surrounding an individual as symbolized by the crystals chosen in divination techniques.

PENDULUM DOWSING

A method of divination which uses a pendulum, usually made of crystal or precious metal, to locate missing objects or to give answers to specific questions. The pendulum cam also be used to dowse for geopathic stress.

PIEZOELECTRIC EFFECT

Discovered by French physicist and chemist Pierre Curie (1859–1906), this effect occurs when mechanical stress is applied to a crystal and an electrical voltage is produced across the crystal's surface.

PROGRAMMING

A term used to describe how to focus specific energy into a crystal so that it continues to promote the energy of your chosen desire.

REINFORCING STONES

Stones which help to restore and enhance energy to a specific chakra energy center.

RESONANCE

Sympathetic vibrations between people, objects, symbols, or qualities, as well as between the crystals you choose and the purpose they are used for.

SPREAD

A way of laying out the stones in a certain pattern so as to create a symbolic matrix for divination.

SUBDUING STONES

Stones which calm and restore balance to an over-active chakra energy center.

TAROT

A deck of seventy-eight mystical cards which are symbolic of the archetypal nature of the universe.

TUMBLED

Stones that have been polished in a large drum with grit to give them a smooth and often shiny finish.

UNIVERSAL ENERGY

The energy which permeates and connects all things. Also known as "anima mundi" in the Neoplatonic system of thought, "ch'i" by the ancient Chinese Taoists, "prana" in Hindu culture, and "mana" in Polynesian cultures.

VIBRATIONAL ENERGY

According to Quantum physics, everything in the Universe moves and vibrates at varying speeds on the electromagnetic spectrum.

FURTHER READING

Hall, Judy.
The Crystal Bible.
Arlesford, UK: Godsfield Press, 2003.

Hall, Judy.
Crystal Healing.
Arlesford, UK: Godsfield Press, 2005.

Hall, Judy.
101 Power Crystals.
Beverly, US: Fair Winds Press, 2011.

Mercier, Patricia.
The Chakra Bible.
New York, US: Sterling, 2007.

Simmons, Robert.
The Pocket Book of Stones.
Berkeley, US: North Atlantic Books, 2015.

Virtue, Doreen.
Crystal Therapy.
London, UK: Hay House Publishing, 2005.

USEFUL WEBSITES

The Astrology Room
www.theastrologyroom.com

The Crystal Healer
www.thecrystalhealer.co.uk

Crystalinks
www.crystalinks.com

Crystal Vaults
www.crystalvaults.com

INDEX